MOVING FORWARD

MOVING FORWARD

A Stickman's Journey of Hope and Meaning

BRIG SORBER

Original Stickman and Founding Member

Forefront
BOOKS

Published by Forefront Books.

Cover Design by Bruce Gore, Gore Studio Inc.
Interior Design by Mary Susan Oleson, Blu Design Concepts

ISBN: 978-1-63763-073-0 print
ISBN: 978-163763-074-7 e-book

TO MY WIFE, FRANCINE.
Thank you for the ferocious support, the love,
the wit, and the occasional kick in the ass.
I would not want to be on this life's ride
with anyone else but you.
I love you.

Contents

A happy life consists not in the absence,
but in the mastery of hardships.

—HELEN KELLER

Introduction

THE UNITED STATES has always been a country on the move. Many of the original North American tribes were nomadic, following the herds that provided their food. In the same way, many of the early immigrants were continually advancing. Often referred to as the first "settlers," they were anything but that. Not content to stay in one place, these individuals were constantly pressing forward in search of new horizons.

That restlessness and sense of adventure continues to run deep in our veins. One-tenth of the population moves to a new home every year. During their lifetime, the average American will move eleven times. Back in the day, people would take with them only what they could carry or load in a covered wagon. Not anymore.

Over the years, Americans have accumulated more possessions, and many need help to get from point A to point B. People on the move are generally at major crossroads in their life, whether that's taking ownership of a dream home or leaving a place of nightmares behind. It comes as no surprise that moving to a new home is one of the most stressful events in a person's life. It's up there with the death of a loved one, divorce, and starting a new job—each of which could also be the reason for moving, only adding to the pressure.

Throughout the years, I have learned a few lessons about how to move things as efficiently and effectively as possible. Personally, I've been on thousands of moves, the first of which I did with my brother, Jon, back in the '80s when we first started hauling people's stuff, a concept my mother would later build into the Two Men and a Truck moving company. In the process of moving, I have also learned a thing or two about moving people forward—in other words, leadership.

I've held many titles in my life. Mover, insurance salesman, warehouse manager, franchisee, franchise developer, president, CEO, husband, and dad—just to name a few—and I've learned leadership lessons in each role.

Though many of these titles differ greatly, they actually have more in common than what we may see on the surface. Each title allows us the ability to show we care by listening, showing compassion, practicing discernment, bringing hope, and showing love.

I have also seen the darker side of leadership: anger, mistrust, intimidation, bullying, and apathy. If you have been around long enough, you have probably experienced most or all these traits. As we age and our careers move forward, many of us accumulate leadership titles. We need to be aware that they come with both a responsibility and an opportunity.

I have learned from my own mistakes over the

years that if we are not careful, we will primarily make decisions to benefit ourselves. We often do this intentionally, but other times subconsciously. It happens when we lean toward what "feels good" or toward what our heart desires. In doing so, we are protecting what is most dear to us: our own egos.

We must find something else to base our decisions on. Something bigger than ourselves. A true north, if you will.

In geography, true north refers to the direction that points precisely toward the geographic north pole. Most people don't realize that magnetic compasses don't point precisely toward true north because magnetic north is almost always out of alignment with true geographic north. They align only every few hundred years. This is important for sailing and navigation because most charts are oriented based on true north. True north is always the same, but magnetic north changes.

If you fail to account for the variation between true north and magnetic north, you may not run into any trouble on a short trip. But on a longer trip, that small deviation can steer you way off course. You can even end up at an entirely different destination.

At a pivotal point in my life, my decisions began to follow my new true north. No more meandering around feelings and perceptions, short-term gains or losses. My growing confidence in my true north allowed more consistency during those defining moments of life, the kind where you have to make important decisions while facing uncertainty.

Having a true north helped me fight against the onslaught of short-term, Monday morning quarterbacks who arise along the way in business. More importantly, a true north direction allowed me to fly above the hurts and hunger of my own ego—which has an insatiable appetite.

A true north direction allows multitasked leaders to be more consistent in managing their titles. Managing my decision-making roles based on emotions and feelings became exhausting—if not overwhelming—to the point I felt like throwing in the towel. This newfound direction not only brought consistency in how I lead others in my different roles but also keeps me moving forward with anticipation and hope in every aspect of my life. We have all experienced traumatic times in our lives, and these painful moments can accumulate and leave us feeling inadequate, shameful, angry, and withdrawn.

Hopeless, if you will.

Even after having tremendous success and achieving all my dreams, I reached a point of hopelessness. But then I made a discovery that changed everything: what if these challenging times were seeds planted by our Creator? From seeds of trauma grow antidotes for our challenges.

INTRODUCTION

In sharing my story, I offer the seeds God planted in me as well as what grew out of them. More importantly, I hope you see the seeds that lie dormant in you and what they could mean if you harvest your crop.

CHAPTER ONE

Is This It?

THE PHONE IN MY OFFICE had been ringing off the hook for the past few days, with people calling to tell me they had seen my picture on Oprah Winfrey's television show.

Someone from her team had contacted us after seeing an article in *The National Enquirer* about our company, Two Men and a Truck. Oprah was planning to air a show on successful start-ups, and she wanted to feature my mom to tell the story of how she had developed standardized processes for the gritty little moving business my younger brother, Jon, and I had started when we were teenagers. My mom, Mary Ellen Sheets, had taken what was basically a stint of after-school odd jobs and transformed them into a legitimate nationwide business.

Unfortunately, Mom was replaced by Jeff Bezos at the last minute. At that time, Amazon was still primarily known as an internet bookseller but their stock had taken off during a surge that would later become known as the dot-com bubble. As an "internet pioneer," Amazon had a compelling story.

Fortunately, our story was also compelling, and the Oprah team still wanted to highlight Mom's accomplishments. They asked us to send video and photos so they could feature us on the show. I had forgotten all about it until the voice mails and emails started pouring in. Some were messages from friends who wanted to congratulate me. Others were from people I hadn't heard from since high school.

Then there were the inquiries from those wanting to know how they could become a Two Men and a Truck franchisee. They had seen a winning formula and wanted to be part of it. The national exposure was worth a fortune in advertising dollars. As the company's franchise development director responsible for signing up new franchisees, I knew this was serious pay dirt.

The experience reminded me of changing to a new lure in the middle of a day out fishing. After hours of monotony, a small change can fill the stringer. One short feature on a TV show and we were slammed with leads.

My life kicked into high gear. There was a liberating feeling, like when you break free from a traffic jam and hit the open road. My homelife was going very well, and things at work were accelerating. The open road was ahead of me in every aspect of life.

In my mind, I had planned a personal celebration for quite some time, choosing a bottle of Johnnie Walker Black for the occasion. I didn't know much about whiskey, but I was aware from ads and movies that guys who drank it were big deals. Now that I was somewhat of a big deal myself, Scotch was good enough for me. I went for the Black because it was a deluxe blend, made for moments like this.

From what I had read, the flavor of the liquor needed to be paired with just the right smoke. A gas station Swisher Sweets wouldn't cut it. I went a few steps up to a Romeo y Julieta cigar. Not quite a Cadillac of smoke, more like a Chevy Impala. It would get me where I wanted to go with at least a *little bit* of style.

It was hard to believe that just a few years prior, I was so broke that I couldn't afford windshield washer fluid for the family's two-tone blue 1987 Toyota Corolla. One hard Michigan winter, I had to pull over every couple of miles, get out of the car in my suit and overcoat, and throw snow on the windshield to remove the road salt.

Now my new off-white, hand-detailed Audi A4 with a light tan leather interior sat in the driveway with a Frank Sinatra CD slotted in the sound system. I felt as though Frank Sinatra epitomized the sort of quiet sophistication and manliness I had long aspired to and finally achieved. My favorite track on the *Strangers in the Night* album—"Summer Wind"—was on automatic replay. It was a love song, really, but the line in which he sang, "The autumn wind and the winter winds, they have come and gone," seemed to capture my mood. I was in the summer of my life.

Along with the family van, the Audi fit in the

two-car garage attached to our well-appointed home. If we had risen in the world with our vehicles, it seemed like we had gone into orbit when it came to our living situation. Our previous house had been such a dump that a relative of ours had suggested we go away for a weekend. He went on to imply that during the weekend, a fire just might break out in the place and provide us with a nice insurance check that we could use to "build a real house." I laughed, but he was dead serious. We didn't take him up on the offer, but there were times when just daydreaming about it was enough to boost my spirits.

The three-bedroom, two-and-a-half-bath brick ranch we had graduated to may not have been grand, but we thought it was great—certainly in comparison to our former home. That house was in one of the older established neighborhoods in Okemos, Michigan. This was a place where a lot of my friends lived when I was growing up. Many of their parents were still there.

Moving into the area myself many years later, I had come prepared. I had been educated early in life about the importance of keeping up outward appearances. At a welcome-to-the-neighborhood party, an older man who lived across the street came over and introduced himself.

"I live over there," he said, pumping my hand. "I just want you to know that we all take good care of our yards here. Good to have you in the neighborhood."

Little did he know that his message was less of a gentle warning than a barefaced challenge. He might as well have walked over, spit chew on my boot, and told me, "Don't bring the neighborhood down, son!" I may have come from a less well-to-do community, but I had learned from my dad always to present a sharp-looking face to the world. From the way a person dressed to how well their yard was cared for, outward appearances mattered. It's not that we were pretentious, but my dad believed that outward appearances communicated a lot about what was on the inside.

Thanks for throwing that log on my fire, old man! I thought, smiling inwardly. *Oh, it's on!*

A year later, that same neighbor came over to congratulate me on how things looked. Using my Polaris Sportsman four-wheeler and a chain, I had ripped out the old overgrown shrubs running wild, replacing them with crisp new flower beds and shrubs. The lawn had been carefully fertilized, seeded, and watered.

The yard was now a lush green with the mowed lines taking on the look of a well-pressed plaid shirt. With three small kids around, it wasn't quite up to golf course standards, but it was the best-looking grass on the street. I had also resurfaced the cracked driveway, tamed the wild trees in the backyard, and added a fire pit off to one side.

We were still riding our wave of celebrity from *The Oprah Winfrey Show* when I got home that day. It was a Thursday evening in the summer of 1998. My wife, Fran, was out running the kids to different activities, so I changed into shorts and a T-shirt and mounted the new John Deere riding mower she had bought me for my birthday. I cut the lawn before edging the sidewalk and driveway. Then I cleaned the pool, enjoying the way the fading sunlight made the water sparkle over the new aqua-green liner we had recently installed.

With everything put away and straightened up, enjoying the aroma of freshly cut grass, I decided this would be the perfect evening to sip that Johnnie Walker and pull out the Romeo y Julieta. I would toast my success and tell myself, *I made it!*

As more of a beer guy, I didn't have any whiskey tumblers in the house, but no way was I going to drink my Black out of one of the kids' milk glasses. Rummaging around in the cupboard, I managed to find a short, chunky glass that would work. I dropped in a couple of ice cubes and poured two fingers of whiskey.

Taking it outside, I settled in a lawn chair near the pool. Savoring the moment, I took my time to clip the cigar, light it, draw in, and exhale slowly. Looking out over our property, I raised the glass to my lips, sipped . . . and gagged. So much for the "hints of sweet vanilla" and "toffee notes" I had anticipated. The whiskey was cold and harsh. I managed not to spit out what was already in my mouth, but as I swallowed I tipped the rest onto the lawn, ice cubes and all.

"Wow, how can people drink that?" I said out loud to myself.

Hope it doesn't kill my grass, I thought.

Having looked forward to this symbolic moment for so long, the reality was disappointing. But I was not going to let that rob me of any self-satisfaction. *I'm still successful*, I told myself. *I'll just find another drink … maybe Pink Squirrels*, I chuckled.

I finished my cigar as I looked around with satisfaction at my yard, my pool, and my house. *I should probably join the country club too*, I decided. I could rub elbows there with other rich guys and we could tell war stories about our businesses. Maybe I could learn more from them about how to better fit into a lifestyle of success.

As I reflected on all that Fran and I had come through—all the sacrifice and grinding it had taken—I had to admit that I expected achieving our goals to be more fulfilling. Maybe it would just take a little time for it all to sink in . . . to adjust to this new level of living, I reasoned. Perhaps, like Johnnie Walker Black, success is an acquired taste.

My reverie ended when Fran and the kids returned home. After we put all three kids into bed, I told Fran that I'd had the whiskey and cigar celebration I had been talking about for some time.

She smiled. "And?"

"It was good," I said, noncommittally, as we headed to bed.

MOVING FORWARD

I woke up the next morning with a sour taste in my mouth. It wasn't from the Johnnie Walker. There was this sickly, hollow feeling that ran deep into my stomach. I showered, hoping the hot water would blast some life into me.

It gave me enough energy to help Fran with our typical morning craziness of getting three kids up, dressed, and fed. Then I headed to the new office Two Men and a Truck had recently built on the edge of town. This location was another sign of how far we had come from our early days when the business was run from our kitchen table and a shed built off my grandma's barn.

Juggling the demands of supporting our existing franchisees while responding to the influx of inquiries from prospective newcomers kept me busy enough, but I was conscious of unease somewhere beneath the surface.

Walking into the house later that day, I was irritated to find things out of place. Though it was important to me for the house to look neat and tidy, I knew that wasn't always realistic when you share a home with four other people and three of them are kids. But that didn't stop me from being quietly ticked off.

As usual, Fran could read what was going on inside. "What's the matter?" she asked.

"Nothing," I snapped. "I'm fine."

24

She knew better, but she also knew that pushing me for more wouldn't help, so she let it slide. I tried to stuff the grumbly feelings down inside, hoping that maybe I'd be back to my usual chipper self after a good night's sleep.

No such luck. If anything, I felt even worse the next morning—like a heaviness was slowly pouring over me, down from my head. I lay in bed trying to make sense of how I was feeling.

Life was good. Things were promising at work, and we were in a sweet season at home. Having weathered some hard times in the early years of our marriage, our increasing financial well-being had taken much of the pressure off. We were doing well in our relationship, we enjoyed a comfortable standard of living, and our children were in a good place. They were doing fine in school, and I was coaching some of their sports teams. All in all, it was the American dream.

But as I got up and got ready for the day, the cloud over me seemed only to grow darker. Somehow, I dragged myself into the office, trying to smile and project my usual bright presence. It was hard work.

During a meeting with a visitor who was presenting the details of an important new software program we were considering, I found myself sitting with my head dropped in my hands. The guy glanced at me with concern as though he thought I was about to throw up. But to his credit, he managed to complete his pitch. Afterward I apologized.

"I'm sorry," I said. "It wasn't you. I'm not feeling right, and I guess I'm just really tired."

He told me it was okay, and I went back to my office. Slumping down in my chair, I thought, *What the hell is wrong with me?* By the time I got home that evening, I had figured it out.

"I've got cancer," I told Fran.

"You *what?*" she said, shocked and confused. "Why would you say that?"

"I need to see a doctor," I said gloomily. "It must be cancer or something like that. There's just no other explanation for me to feel the way I do. It's the classic story you read about all the time—we've worked our asses off to get where we are, and just as we get to enjoy life, we find out one of us has a terminal disease. Why else would I be feeling like this?"

Fran gave me a look of annoyance. "I'll set you an appointment," she said.

Sitting in the doctor's office a day or so later, I ran through my symptoms—or lack of them, more accurately. No fever, no nausea, no aches and pains, no recent accidents of any kind. And yet I felt as if I had been hit by a truck—listless, lifeless, and most of all, hopeless.

The doctor gave me a routine examination. It had been a while since I had exercised regularly because I was so busy with work and the family. Despite that, I was still in relatively good shape.

"Well, you seem to be healthy to me, without giving you a full-blown physical," the doctor said. Then he started to ask about how things were going at work and at home. Stress was often an issue for guys in my stage of life, he told me.

"Life's great, to be honest," I said. "Work is busy, but it's going well, and I love what I do. I don't feel like I am under any pressure there. And things are fine at home too. Family is good. I don't have any reason to feel the way I do. I just don't get it."

The doctor said that he thought I was dealing with depression. He reached for a pad and scribbled a prescription. "Here," he said, "take these and see what they do for you."

I jammed the paper into my wallet and went home. I'd had some experience with hopelessness in the past— the bleak feeling that things were bad and were only going to get worse. But I knew that what I was feeling at that moment wasn't the same. It was more like despair, the sense that things were good and yet somehow that didn't really matter anymore.

In the book of Proverbs, Solomon stated, "Whoever trusts in his riches will fall, but the righteous will flourish like a green leaf" (11:28 ESV). In this simple nugget of wisdom, Solomon described the ultimate failure of any individual who finds their greatest sense of hope in what they have in their wallet. Or in titles. Or social status. These things are not inherently bad, but when their pursuit consumes our hearts and time, we lose what is important in life. We lose what God intends for us.

I told Fran about my appointment and noted that I wasn't going to get the prescription filled. I did not make this decision lightly. Depression is real, and I knew people who needed medication to balance the chemical makeup of their bodies. But I felt strongly that my situation was different. The change was too abrupt. One day I was fine; the next day everything went dark.

"I need to get to the bottom of this," I said. "I'm not just going to bury it. I want to find out what's wrong." When I told Fran about the doctor asking whether I work out, she suggested I start lifting again.

After dinner, I went downstairs to the basement. I had a decent workout room set up down there—an Olympic bar set, a bench, and a range of dumbbells. I had used it quite a bit in the past, and I remembered how good it felt. Maybe pumping some iron and shedding some sweat would dislodge the feeling of heaviness.

I fitted a forty-five-pound plate to each end of the bar, enough to get my blood flowing and my muscles working. I lay down, centered myself under the bar, and reached up to grasp it. I thought I'd pump out ten or fifteen quick reps to get things started.

But as soon as I gripped the bar, I felt the strength leak out of me like air from a balloon. I dropped my arms, cupped my hands over my face, and began to sob. Tears spilled out of my eyes and down my face. It went on for several minutes.

This unexpected reaction really got my attention. I hadn't cried like that since I was a kid and for what?

Not wanting to worry Fran any further, I pulled myself together and wiped my face before I went back upstairs. With all sorts of questions spinning around in my head, I went through the motions of helping Fran with the kids, hoping that somehow things might be better the next day.

Unfortunately, I awoke to more of the same—heaviness, hopelessness, and a sense that everything was meaningless. I had achieved everything I ever hoped for, and it didn't amount to anything. A sense of eagerness and expectation had always fueled my workdays, but that motivation was gone. It was as though I had clawed and climbed my way to the top of the ladder of success, only to look around and think, *So, this is all there is? Really? This is what I worked for?*

The morning was cloudy as I drove to the office, appropriate for my mood. Before diving into the day's schedule, I checked my email inbox and then had a quick look at the news online. As I browsed, something in an advertisement caught my eye—something that would lead me to throw away the prescription in my wallet and change my life in ways I could not even begin to imagine.

CHAPTER TWO

Run with Purpose

Parenting was approached differently when I was growing up. Back then, most parents had a hands-off mentality when it came to their kids. Today many of us helicopter over our children's school, athletic, and social activities, mowing down every obstacle they face.

As kids, we weren't tethered to our cell phones or tracked by GPS. The only phone in most homes hung in the kitchen attached to a twenty-foot coiled cord. Anyone who wanted privacy had to stretch the cord behind the nearest door.

Our town was crisscrossed with dirt trails from countless years of kids' bike traffic. When we played baseball, there was always a pile of bikes behind the benches. Parents would drive to the games and very few players rode with their parents.

Years later, I coached my kids on those same fields, and it was evident the world had changed. There were no more bikes piled up behind the benches, and the dirt trails were all grown over. The world is faster now, kids are more tightly managed, and it's viewed as irresponsible when younger kids are out riding bikes without parental supervision.

When I was in school, test scores were not instantly sent to our parents. And the only place to be bullied was at school or the bus stop. Now the bullying continues wherever your smartphone is, even at home.

As a small boy, I felt overlooked—lost somewhere in the middle of my parents' busy lives. That kind of thing happened very easily back then. It's not that there weren't any fun times. I remember family movie nights with Mom making homemade fudge. There were camping trips on Lake Michigan or in Michigan's Upper Peninsula, the U.P.

One of my most traumatic childhood memories was a consistent stutter that started around first grade and lasted for several years. My parents did not helicopter in to help or coddle me but instead pushed me to deal with it. That was not an easy task for a seven-year-old, but their approach did make me work to improve myself. Though unspoken, the message was that I had to toughen up. These matter-of-fact lessons from my parents continued into my preteen years.

When I was about twelve, we visited a farm belonging to one of my parents' friends. A big storm blew through. I was in the barn with the other kids, and we all ran to the house. I was flailing my arms and legs, trying to keep up. Mom took me aside, "Brig, don't ever run like that again." She continued, "Pump your arms and move your legs. Run with purpose."

Strangely enough, this rebuke didn't upset me. Instead, it made me feel cared for and loved. I actually liked it. So much so that I never forgot Mom's words, and as I got older I applied them to other situations in my life. *Quit flailing! Run with purpose.*

More than anything, I wanted my dad's attention and affirmation, but it was hard to earn. He often seemed distracted or irritated, and I often felt like a disappointment to him. Knowing how important athletics were to my dad, I thought I might be able to win his approval by following in his footsteps.

Dad's youthful glory days were over, but he still carried himself with the confidence of a star athlete. He had a presence that others noted, which made me proud of him. I became the ball boy for the team he played on, the Diamond Reo fastpitch softball team. The other players had a lot of respect for him, and I enjoyed the reflected glory of being his son.

Though small for my age, I did have good hand–eye coordination and decided to try out for a baseball team. Another boy on our street belonged to a team with actual uniforms. Their names were displayed across the back of their jerseys, just like the pros. I wanted more than anything to be part of a real team.

I badgered Dad into inquiring about me joining the team. Finally, he took me to the coach's house, where the man hit a couple of ground balls to me in his backyard while Dad watched. Despite my best efforts, the coach looked over at my dad and said simply, "He's really not that good."

"Yeah," Dad said. "I didn't think he was."

My dad's words stung. I hadn't won Dad's approval. He didn't sugarcoat things, and while I was crushed at that moment, I now understand an important take-away from the experience. Even though my dad knew I wasn't good enough, at least he took me to the coach's house and gave me a chance. Of course, I didn't see it that way at the time.

Shortly after that, I began comparing my life to my friends', especially their family dynamics. I spent as much time as I could hanging out at my friends' homes observing how their parents were more involved in their lives. I envied their stability.

In contrast, some of my friends were jealous of my freedom. Even when I was young, I was allowed to come and go pretty much when I wanted. That hands-off parenting style only deepened when I became a teenager, especially after Mom and Dad broke up.

As part of my desire for a sense of belonging, I joined the Cub Scouts. Unfortunately, my time there ended prematurely when I locked the den mother in a closet—she didn't think it was as funny as I did.

My stint in uniform did give me one of a handful of special memories with Dad. He helped me make my Pinewood Derby race car and gave it a stylish paint job. I still have that little car, and it serves as a reminder to invest in my own kids' experiences.

With my parents' work and other commitments, my sister, Melanie, my brother, Jon, and I all spent a lot of time in the care of babysitters or grandparents. When we were old enough, we looked after ourselves. That led to some formative experiences of their own.

Neither Mom nor Dad had a serious churchgoing background, but for some reason they selected a fiercely religious babysitter around the time I was eight years old. Monday through Friday, we were dropped off at her house early in the morning. Then we were ushered into the basement, where we were made to lie on the floor under a blanket until it was time to go to school.

She was a strict older woman with a tight-lipped, angry scowl who quoted the Bible in lecturing tones. She didn't believe in sparing the rod, though her version was one of those paddles with a rubber ball broken off. She also had a bar of soap for washing out smart-talking young mouths, which my younger brother, Jon, experienced more than once.

Each summer, she hosted a Bible camp for the neighborhood kids. She talked at length about how much Jesus loved the world. It never made sense to me how a loving Jesus could turn this lady so sour. I had no interest in getting to know the God she talked about having a personal relationship with.

He seemed angry and disapproving, and I wondered how big His paddle was.

These were the influences I had around me, which is probably why I was happiest in the care of our grandparents. I especially enjoyed my time with Grandpa Eberly, who was usually dressed in green work pants and a white T-shirt, often bearing a stain from Grandma Eberly's strawberry shortcake made with fresh strawberries from their garden.

Grandpa Eberly taught me much about living life on purpose. He did this not through instruction but through a few very simple actions, so profound they've impacted my personal and professional success as much as anything else I've learned.

I think Grandpa Eberly realized I was hungry to know that I really mattered to someone. In his quiet way, he tried to fill that gap. He always had time for me, inviting me to sit with him in front of that old Sears house he had purchased as a kit from a catalog.

The house kit showed up on a train in downtown Lansing. He purchased his three-and-a-half-acre piece of land for a dollar from his dad and dug the basement with a team of horses and a shovel. The western border of the property was on the Red Cedar River. It wasn't a big tract of land. Still, he made the most of it, planting cherry trees, apple trees, and flowers. He also had a vegetable garden where he grew asparagus, tomatoes, string beans, cucumbers, potatoes, watermelons, raspberries, and strawberries.

Grandpa grew pumpkins well over one hundred

pounds and gave them to us grandkids. It would take everything my dad had to lift them out of the trunk of his car and put them on our porch. Grandpa and Grandma would sell their produce at a self-serve roadside stand, using the annual proceeds to buy us Christmas presents.

Occasionally, Grandpa and I would sit side-by-side on summer evenings under the canopy of an old maple tree. He would smoke his signature unfiltered Camel cigarettes in his strawberry-stained T-shirt as we listened to Ernie Harwell's iconic voice giving us the play-by-play of the Detroit Tigers' games.

Harwell would compete with the AM radio static caused by the heat lightning on those hot summer nights. To this day, when a radio crackles, it takes me back to those nights when approaching rain clouds would interrupt the broadcast. If only I could have bottled those moments.

Grandpa wasn't a big man, but he made a big impact, and not just on my life. I couldn't believe how many people turned out for his funeral to honor him when lung cancer took him at sixty-nine. He taught me that you don't have to make a big deal about making a difference—just give people your attention. Grandpa made me feel like I mattered. I remember talking to him about an irritating kid who was on my basketball team in fifth grade.

"That kid sounds like a real shit," Grandpa said.

It was the first and, I believe, the only time I heard my grandpa swear. He validated my feelings because he sensed my frustration, and he spoke to me like an adult.

Grandpa was always fearful I was going to drown while fishing at my friend's cottage. Twice he talked to me at length about wearing a life jacket. I could see the concern on his face and hear it in his voice. Where some kids may have thought this needless worry talk was an annoyance, I loved it.

Several years after Grandpa passed away, my grandma was placed in a nursing home. My mom spent many months going through the little Sears house, the old chicken coop, and the pole barn. She told us kids everything had been sorted. "Take one last look because anything left is going to the dump," she announced with a sense of finality.

I walked through the house and was flooded with memories of several Thanksgiving Day dinners and Christmas Eve parties that will go down as my happiest childhood memories. The house seemed smaller with all the furniture gone and the pictures off the walls.

I walked through the yard and noticed it had lost all the detail and beauty my grandparents poured into it. The bushes were overgrown and the flower-beds were choked with weeds. I looked in the chicken coop and found several of Grandpa's yard tools. He had painted the wood handles an orange color and the metal heads green—a number two shovel, a coal shovel, a posthole digger, and a hard rake. I took them all and still have them.

When I walked into the pole barn, I was shocked to see several Christmas ornaments lying in a pile of trash on the floor. One caught my eye: a light blue paper Christmas wreath. I remembered it from countless Christmas seasons when it hung over the fireplace.

I picked it up and was surprised to discover it was made of computer punch cards. Each one was carefully folded, stapled, painted light blue with spray paint, and then touched up with glue and glitter. It was amazing that something most would look at and deem worthless had etched a memory I will never forget.

The pile on the floor had other memories, mostly cheap five-and-dime store items I thought were priceless as a child. I realized something important in that moment. It wasn't the item that mattered but the love and care poured into each of us by my grandparents.

I walked out of the barn as the wind whistled through the open door and the tree branches. With the holiday memories flooding my mind, I stopped and gazed at the plot of land my grandparents had carved out for their lives over the years. What seemed like endless acres when I was a kid only looked like someone's larger-than-average yard now.

My reflections seemed sad until I put it in perspective. Nothing stays the same. People come and go, and time moves on. People dream and then work hard to make their dreams a reality. When their time is done, so is their reality.

Life is no different from a child's day at the beach. A child can take hours to build a sandcastle, sweating every detail, but when the father says it's time to go, the child must leave. Over time, wind and waves take down the sandcastle, and the next day a new child shows up to build a completely different castle with the same sand. This happens over and over.

As adults, we build our lives, our businesses, and our homes. We came into this world naked—with nothing—and we will leave the same way. Just as the child left the sweat equity poured into the sandcastle when her father called, we must do the same when our Father calls us home. Our wealth and equity will be left for others, and the cycle will continue.

When I climbed into my truck to go home, I realized the biggest thing I took from Grandpa wasn't his yard tools but the time he carved out for me while building his life. He listened, he understood my feelings, and he cared.

With my open-door policy at our corporate office and my dealings with the franchisees over the years, Grandpa's simple communication and interpersonal skills have been very valuable. People often come to me to vent. It's good to listen and remember that these are people with their own hopes and dreams, not just business associates and employees.

Grandpa Eberly taught me the most valuable lesson about how to run with purpose: Life is really about other people. If your life is not centered on others, it will be hollow, empty, and probably not very successful. But if you want to make a lasting impact while achieving your dreams, put others first. Connect first as humans. Validate their issues. When you can sense their trust and gain an understanding of how they feel, the conversation can then move forward. Grandpa Eberly did not walk me through this point by point—he simply lived it in front of me.

Take time for other people. Many people in today's world are starved for attention and human interaction. Smartphones, social media, and most recently COVID have led to an epidemic of loneliness and isolation.

Due to the impersonal and sometimes harsh approach of many adults in the 1970s, my grandpa enjoyed daily opportunities to impact the world around him by doing little things. How many people can you impact today by simply taking time to listen and respond with care and respect?

CHAPTER THREE

A Worker in Progress

IT CAN TAKE SEVERAL tributaries to form a river, and the same is true with leadership. My first leadership tributary was the equivalent of water bubbling out of the mud. I was eight years old, trying to land my first job that was more than just a relative giving me a chore. Dragging my rake down a leaf-covered sidewalk on a drizzly afternoon, I started ringing doorbells.

The first three doorbells I rang went unanswered. Then I hit the jackpot. A man answered the door and asked what I wanted. I stammered through my sales pitch and asked if I could rake his front yard for a dollar. He looked over his shoulder at another man behind him. The second man said, "Sure, go ahead."

Excited, I set to work. As I built a large pile of leaves on the lawn, I noticed the men were busy moving things from the house into their car before eventually driving off. I kept working, figuring they would be back soon with my dollar. Not too long after, another vehicle pulled in. A confused man got out and asked me what I was doing.

"I'm raking the leaves," I told him.

"Who told you to do that?" he replied.

"The man who answered the door," I said. "I asked

him if I could do it for a dollar, and the guy with him said go ahead."

The man disappeared inside the house only to come out a few minutes later when a police car pulled into the driveway. *I did nothing wrong by raking leaves,* I thought. The policeman spoke with the man, then asked me a few questions about the guys in the house. Eventually he left and the man went back in the house.

I remember feeling aggravated because I was so excited to finish the job and get my dollar. I raked for another twenty minutes or so and knocked on the door to collect payment.

"I'm finished," I said.

He looked at me, exasperated. "This is my house. I did not ask you to rake my leaves. I just got robbed!"

We stood for a brief, quiet moment staring at each other. I was too young to comprehend his issue. There was a neat pile of leaves in his yard, and I expected payment for services rendered. He broke the tension by sighing and pulling his wallet out from his back pocket.

"Here you go, buddy." He handed me a worn dollar bill.

I was so excited to tell my family, I practically floated home, clutching the first dollar I had ever earned on my own initiative. It was as if I had caught my first fish all by myself. I met Mom in the kitchen and recounted every detail of how I made my first dollar.

She interrupted me, "Brig, you walked into some-one's house while it was being robbed!" I had already put that much together, but the bigger story to me was the dollar I had earned.

Mom's voice sounded concerned, but she also seemed satisfied that I took the initiative to make money. Looking back on the drama surrounding my first dollar, I wish I could find the man who gave this little kid a buck after what happened to him. I would buy him a beer.

By the time I was a teenager, I entered my first business partnership. Tim Vollmer was a good friend from school, and we decided to go into the lawn mowing business together. Neither of us was old enough to drive, so we'd pull our lawn mowers behind our bikes to every job.

We calculated how much money we wanted to make per week and what to charge per job. Next we determined how many mowing jobs were required to meet our weekly goal. Pretty simple math.

We began by turning to the whitepages and finding all the Okemos addresses. We cold-called people and introduced them to our new lawn mowing service. We booked five out of the first eight names in the directory. I couldn't believe how easy this was.

Tim and I were flying high that summer. We were independent, spending time in the sun, and making just enough money to support everything we wanted to do. After the lawns were mowed for the day, we would drop the mowers at home and play Frisbee at the park on Lake Lansing. On windy days, we would sail my parents' old Hobie Cat.

Mowing lawns wasn't my only income generator. I also got a job at Philipelli's, an Italian restaurant in our hometown. The pay wasn't great, but there were perks. An untouched half of a pizza was often brought back to the kitchen, and I would set it aside for later. Occasionally I would enjoy a half-pitcher of beer someone had failed to finish. Quite often, there was some form of free entertainment that went along with the job. With such a large student clientele, frequent hijinks ensued, typically fueled by alcohol.

My work life took off once I learned to drive. Dad had bought a beat-up 1966 Ford truck from my Uncle Norm for a couple hundred dollars. Dad would use this truck on weekends for miscellaneous projects. After it sat in our driveway for over a year, I told Dad I would fix up the truck if he would let me have it. He agreed.

This was before pickup trucks became cool. I didn't care, not even about the hole in the floorboard by my left foot where I could see the road racing underneath. That truck was priceless to me, and it opened new horizons.

First, it gave me greater freedom. I could come and go as I pleased. Instead of pedaling my bike or being dropped off by my parents, I drove to Philipelli's for work. What a thrill that was. During my first evening shift, I took the trash out more than usual just so I could stare at my truck parked in the lot.

Having a truck also made life easier for Tim and me since we could throw our mowers in the back. The transportation also helped expand our business. Tim's father, Ray, came to us with a proposition. He owned a real estate company and offered us five more lawns to mow at properties he was selling. We were on a roll.

Lastly, having a truck enabled me to get a job delivering the *Wheeler Dealer* ad paper to local neighborhoods. My friends and I got paid cash for distributing the weekly publication to less-desirable areas of Lansing.

All this work wasn't just padding my wallet—it was also building my self-esteem. I didn't think about the bigger questions of life at the time. I just liked the way work made me feel. Later I realized that what I learned working those jobs influenced who I became.

Proverbs states, "A slack hand causes poverty, but the hand of the diligent makes rich" (10:4 ESV). In a later chapter, it says, "The hand of the diligent will rule, while the slothful will be put to forced labor" (12:24 ESV).

The wording of these scriptures may seem out of date but their meaning is relevant. I find it amazing that these verses are over three thousand years old.

Looking back, I should have found comfort in the fact that the antidote for many of life's challenges, such as poverty, is this: work always.

Being able to buy whatever I needed with my own money made me feel more independent. I loved what the 1966 Ford represented. It was a little rough around the edges but it was dependable. We were a good fit.

On occasion, my friends' parents would comment on my work ethic. They loved how we used my old '66 Ford to hustle for work. It felt good to be validated. One evening I drove over to a friend's house for a party. I came straight from work and was a little late arriving. When my friend greeted me, she said, "My mom says you're going to be a millionaire one day."

I looked at her, shocked. "Me? Why?"

"Because you work so hard at a young age," she told me. I shrugged it off, as if she had told me I was going to be a professional baseball player when I grew up. However, her words stayed with me.

My first moving job involved one of our parents' income properties. They were forced to evict a tenant who was months overdue on his rent, and they wanted Jon and me to help clear the place out.

When we arrived with my truck, the sheriff was on hand to ensure everything went without incident.

The sheriff was standing there, idly flipping through a *Hustler* magazine among the tenant's possessions as we carried his things to the curb. When the tenant showed up, the sheriff said whatever he didn't take would be taken by neighbors, and whatever was left would be taken to the dump. Dad told me to go back the next day, load anything that was left into my truck, and then take it to the dump.

This was my first move that didn't include yard waste.

I found it easier and cleaner to move miscellaneous household items than yard debris. Plus, there were more of these jobs, so I started looking for more work in this lucrative field.

Brent Webster was a friend I fished and golfed with. Soon we were hauling junk together and calling ourselves B & B Hauling. It was more of a joke. We had no signage or business cards. We posted a single piece of paper with tear-off numbers at the local grocery store, and word-of-mouth was our only advertising.

We would cram anything we could fit into the box of my old Ford and take it to the dump. However, B & B Hauling dissolved when Brent and I went off to college. A few summers later, Brent worked with Two Men and a Truck from time to time when the company evolved.

When I was eighteen years old, I sold my truck and detached from the moving business altogether. My brother, Jon, along with one of his friends, began doing moves using his friend's truck. Not long after, our mother got involved and bought a used twelve-foot box van to replace the pickup truck.

The tributaries weaving through my life's journey were starting to flow for the company that would later become Two Men and a Truck. When I came home from college on semester breaks, Jon and I would use Mom's old step van for moving jobs.

Some customers would get upset when we arrived because we were so small. This continued to haunt me during my entire moving career. Their disappointment started with a concerned look as they met us at the front door. But I learned to tackle their disappointment head-on.

"Is there a problem, ma'am?" one of us would ask. "You look upset."

"Well, we thought we were paying for two men. We were expecting big, strapping lads, but—not to sound mean—we got you."

"Ma'am, I understand," I answered. "How about we work for fifteen minutes, and if you feel we are not up to it, just let us know and we will call the office and have them send some bigger guys."

"That's fair."

We were walking a tightrope without a net because there was no office and there were no bigger guys. Meanwhile, we would have already walked the house and mentally loaded everything onto the truck. We would start by heading for one of the biggest pieces to be moved—typically the freezer down in the basement.

Those big freezers were the items homeowners could not budge. They were like the black hole of the household. If a dropped pen or a matchbox car rolled underneath them, they would never be seen again.

People's jaws dropped when they saw us pad, strap, and haul one up the stairs in no time, just Jon and me. Practice made perfect, and we regularly moved several freezers a week. By the time we flipped a La-Z-Boy over our shoulders and walked out with it as though it was nothing, we knew an apology was coming and, in most cases, a nice tip.

We learned that the best way to set up a successful move was to put the customer at ease. After all, we were there to provide a service, to solve a problem they could not solve for themselves. As we accumulated more and more moves, we learned valuable tricks of the trade by moving difficult items such as grandfather clocks, grand pianos, and hide-a-bed couches. But we also learned about people.

I found out early that a person's most prized possession may not be what you think. It's not always based on monetary value. After our introduction, I would reassure the customer that we would take care of every item as if they were our own, and then I would pose this question: "Is there one item in particular you are most concerned about?"

In many cases there was. We would hear something like, "My great grandma's old foot pedal sewing machine. It is very fragile and means a lot to our family."

I would nod and ask if she would like to hear how we were going to take care of the sewing machine. I would then explain in detail how the item would be padded and strapped before being placed on top of another moving pad. I would also let her know where it would be placed in the truck and explain the items that would be surrounding it and why. The customer may not have needed to know all that, but the confidence and courtesy in my voice let them know we could be trusted.

People's personalities were as diverse as the items we moved. Some people liked to talk. They would give us a brief history of the items we were moving. They asked about our personal lives and the history of our business. We could have a conversation while we worked. They liked to hear our chatter as we filled the truck and emptied their home.

Other people were all business, no chit-chat or wasted words. Do what you came here to do—no talking on my dime. Often people started quiet and as they saw us work, they loosened up and began to talk.

We always encountered good stories. We might move an older couple out of a house they had lived in for fifty years and into an assisted living facility. Our next move might involve helping a woman who was escaping an abusive relationship. Whatever the situation, we learned to listen.

A good mover will try to offer hope through a calming word or light humor. In some cases, just wearing a gentle smile and remaining silent is a form of comfort. There is an art to reading people and adjusting to them. As my moving career advanced, setting people at ease became my favorite part of the job.

On occasion, we were looked at as less than people, treated as third-class citizens—people who were not smart enough to hold a "real job." I picked up two important nuggets from these encounters. First, continue to work your hardest for them and know that this person's perception is not reality. And second, never treat anyone as if they are less than you, no matter how successful you may become in this world.

Genesis 1:27 states, "So God created man in his own image, in the image of God he created him; male and female he created them" (ESV). All humans have value and purpose because they are created in the image of God. I believe that includes movers too.

CHAPTER FOUR

Finding the Right Teammates

SUPERHEROES MOSTLY SAVE the world single-handedly. Needing assistance is often conveyed as a sign of weakness in novels, movies, or comic books, but that's fantasy. Real life is a team sport. While I may have led the way in launching the Two Men and a Truck ship out into the deep blue water, I no more did that solo than Neil Armstrong took himself to the moon.

I discovered the power of buddying up at an early age. Often feeling alone as a kid, I sought company from friends and their families. Being part of something was important to me. Maybe because I lacked self-confidence, I wanted to surround myself with a team. For whatever reason, I worked better in groups.

I realized that it was important to associate with people who made me want to be better. Like many teenagers, I did rebellious things such as smoking a little pot but quickly decided it wasn't for me. I saw how the smart and athletic kids at school who got into drugs and alcohol went downhill fast—I wanted no part of that.

Given that experience, I should have seen the warning signs when I got involved with the wrong crowd during my early days at Northern Michigan

University. I lost my way for a time because I wanted community—to be a part of something. I prioritized acceptance from others over the acceptability of their standards and behavior.

The group I found my way into had a low regard for education and a high commitment to entertainment—drinking, drugs, and partying. I had long enjoyed alcohol within reason. But at this time in my life, my consumption started to get out of hand.

I also went back to experimenting with pot. Then I started going beyond the occasional communal joint. Though I'd promised myself I would never join the hardcore drug users, it wasn't too long before I was dangling on the edge of that slippery slope. I tried cocaine a few times. It left me feeling emotionally weak, physically hollow, and with a strong sense of guilt.

To make matters worse, the relationship I had been in was in trouble. My girlfriend had cheated on me, leaving me feeling inadequate and rejected. Numbing myself with drugs and alcohol didn't help—I only felt more miserable. On top of that, my grades were suffering to the point where I was put on academic probation.

At the end of my sophomore year, I limped—no, dragged myself—like Quasimodo home for summer vacation. I knew something needed to change but I didn't know what. I felt hopeless. In my eyes, I was becoming a failure.

During the school year, I had seen guys wearing green and gold Northern Michigan University rugby coats. Not knowing a thing about rugby, I dismissed it—until I saw a bumper sticker that read, "Give Blood, Play Rugby."

The humor caught my attention so I decided to check out the last game of the spring season on a warm (above thirty-two degrees) Saturday morning. It changed my life. There were a hundred or so fans either standing or sitting in old lawn chairs with coolers by their sides. The field had six inches of icy snow with long mud puddles running along both sidelines. As the sun beat down and the day warmed up, the field morphed into a muddy slush.

There was an electrifying party atmosphere. Finals were almost complete, there was cold beer, and the sun was melting snow that had been on the ground since late October. Everybody was wearing sunglasses and bouncing with excitement. The Northern Michigan University players wore their traditional black shorts, jerseys with gold and green stripes, and matching socks. These uniforms became so muddy that only by the players' faces could people make out who was on what team.

A player from the University of Wisconsin–Green Bay broke free and ran down the sideline. Two of our Northern Michigan University players tackled him with such force that all three slid uncontrollably in the mud and out of bounds, taking out several fans, coolers, and chairs like bowling pins. The players got up and scrambled back onto the pitch, leaving muddy bodies, beer cans, hats, and gloves strewn on the ground like a makeshift yard sale.

With a broad smile on my face, I thought, *Oh, shit! I want in!* (Though I have tempered my language from my college rugby days, my vocabulary can still be salty at times, as you will see in this book.)

I had three months to transform my body and shake off this funk. My goal was to sign up in the fall. I landed a job at a tool and die shop that summer. The only problem was that the job was on the night shift, working with a skeleton crew made up of five older guys who were all welders or painters. It kept me from hanging out with my friends and seeing my family. Working nights would flip my world upside down.

That summer I learned to be comfortable being alone. I reveled in my independent life. I had a mission: get into the best shape of my life to play rugby in the fall. At work, I wore a navy blue one-piece union suit. I ran a shot blaster and a metal grinder. I came home in the early morning hours with my face and arms black. The whites of my eyes sparkled when I smiled at myself in the mirror. I loved it.

When I got up in the morning, I pounded weights and ran. Day in and day out, I lifted weights, worked, and slept. My body morphed. I felt hope again. I was in control. Control of what? I was not sure—but I was in control.

One morning while in a deep sleep, I was awakened by my mom calling my name. I jumped out of bed, thinking something was wrong. She told me that she just wanted to wake me up and say hi. She reminded me that, with our summer schedules flipped, we lived in the same house but had not seen each other in over two weeks. She was right. We both shared a good laugh.

As that summer started to wind down, my thoughts returned to Northern Michigan University. I was going back a different person—in the best shape of my life mentally and physically. I would take on something new in rugby and fix something broken: my grades. I turned a corner that summer that altered my life.

I returned to campus and while picking up my class schedule, I walked by all the booths that showcased student activities. I found what I was looking for—the Northern Michigan University rugby booth. I got the information I needed where the first practice was and what I should bring.

When I showed up, there were fifty guys already there. After stretching, our coach ran us through some drills and lined us up to run forty-yard sprints. I finished in the top three over and over. I was shocked. I had never been fast before, but the weight training had changed my body.

I didn't know anything about the game but was a fast learner, finding rugby to be much less stop and start and more free-flowing than football. Starting on the wing, then moving to fullback, I ended up at fly-half, a central position in the game.

Rugby is as bruising as American football, minus all the pads. Hence the popular bumper sticker, "Give Blood, Play Rugby!"

Thankfully, in my two and a half years of playing, I never suffered more than a concussion—which I earned trying to bring down a giant-sized lineman whose one thigh was larger than my entire body. He literally ran over my five-foot, eight-inch frame, flattening me out like a cartoon character. Needless to say, I lost that encounter. Our captain had to walk me to my position several times during a ten-minute span. Once the stars stopped spinning, I recovered my focus and was good to go.

Some of the other guys were not so lucky. One of them suffered a gruesome facial wound after getting raked across the face by someone's cleats—you could see his tongue through his gaping cheek. On a couple of occasions, we had guys almost drown when the scrum collapsed into a puddle with a player at the bottom, face submerged in the muddy water.

The other team aside, sometimes the elements

were enough of a challenge themselves. Icy, compacted snow has the consistency of sandpaper when you get tackled and dragged across it dressed in shorts.

Harsh playing conditions simply came with the Upper Peninsula territory.

Often our team would borrow forty-five sets of snowshoes from the Northern Michigan University Outdoor Recreation Center so we could stomp down the pitch after a spring snowstorm the evening before a match. The visiting team would arrive at the pitch with their jaws dropped. They would exclaim, "Are we playing here?"

"Oh, hell yeah," we would say. "Either this or in a cloud of mosquitoes when the snow is gone. Trust us . . . the snow is a better choice!"

It wasn't just sharing in a bruising struggle that drew me to these guys. The bond of brotherhood carried into the rest of our lives from studying to socializing. We were often found sitting in the same corner of the library, trading friendly insults as we read our textbooks.

And of course, like many rugby clubs, we were well-known on campus for our party antics. There were times when we could become a bit boorish, but for the most part, there was an innocence about our pranks that was attractive to some girls (or so we thought).

Rugby was way more manageable than the drugs and hard alcohol of my past. I found my rugby brothers at a good place in my life. We practiced, played, traveled, studied, sang, and drank. Many of us lived together. We became instrumental in one another's lives.

Good friends can make a profound difference in your life, but it doesn't mean they'll stay around forever. Some are there for a season, and then it may be time to gratefully let them go and move on.

* * *

No single person has been more influential in my life than Fran. We met as she was walking with friends past my rugby teammate's house. We were outside grilling on a cool, cloudy fall Saturday. I asked if the girls wanted to join us, and they actually stopped!

Fran and I hit it off immediately. She was a newcomer to Northern Michigan, having transferred from a college in Duluth, Minnesota. Fran was trim and blonde, with the most piercing green eyes I had ever seen. While we were drinking beers and getting to know each other, two of my roommates, Tom Wilson and Ron Doe, pulled up.

"Hey, Brig," Tom yelled, getting out. "Get in! It's time to go back and get ready for the night." With that, he picked me up, opened the rear door, and tossed me inside. As the car pulled away, I managed to right myself. Laughing, I rolled down the window and leaned my head out. "Fran! I'm going to marry you someday!" I called as we drove off. She shook her head with a dismissive laugh.

From my earliest interactions with Fran, I could see a solidness about her that I did not possess. She was quietly confident. I began to understand where all of that came from one day that winter. I woke up to a whiteout, and the snow was heavy enough to cancel classes. This was a cause for celebration and an earlier than usual start to drinking. Wanting to do more with the day than just party, I decided to go over to Fran's and see if she would like to go cross-country skiing.

When Fran welcomed me into her apartment, I first noticed the neatness and orderly manner of everything. Her tidy apartment was in complete contrast to our "guy's house" that looked and smelled like a dump. Our bathtub was so nasty that we would leave messages with our big toe in the black gunk on our shower floor, where months of rugby-field mud had accumulated. I also realized immediately that Fran didn't have much, and most of it wasn't new. Her stuff was well cared for but well-worn.

I understood more when a photograph caught my attention. There were so many people in it that I assumed it was a family reunion. But no, Fran told me it was just a family photo—her mom and dad with her and thirteen brothers and sisters.

By comparison, my upbringing had been a breeze. Fran was the twelfth child born to a couple in Ironwood, the westernmost city in Michigan on the Wisconsin state line. They had squeezed into a three-bedroom house with one bathroom. Fran's dad and brothers added to the house over time, but space was always at a premium. Sharing a bedroom with several sisters left Fran with little quiet time for studying. When she was older, Fran would wait until everyone was in bed, go into the bathroom, lower the toilet seat, and use a clothes hamper as a makeshift desk to do her schoolwork.

I discovered how strong Fran's family ties still were as she went through the photo identifying everyone in the family for me. She pointed out her sister Diane and the baby she was holding.

"That's Michelle, and she means the world to me," Fran said. "And if anything ever happens to Diane, I am going to raise her." It was not a boast, just a matter-of-fact statement that really stood out to me. I had never thought much about kids. To me, they were just small people who got in the way of adults. But family truly mattered to Fran. I was impressed by her selflessness.

We left her apartment and skied out to Presque Isle on Lake Superior, where Fran impressed me by her cross-country skiing ability. She turned out to be better than me, which made sense when I found out she had won several medals in high school. Fran had also run track in high school in addition to playing basketball and volleyball. I struggled to keep up with her as we set out into the blizzard blowing across the lake.

It soon became apparent that Fran was different from other girls I had been around. She was paying her way through school and juggling two or three different jobs along with her studies. I liked her grit. Having always been a diligent student, Fran was able to help me up my game academically. We began to meet in the library to do homework and with her help, my grades improved.

One major step forward in our relationship was me learning to be vulnerable in front of her—a big hurdle for someone who was used to putting on a good front for others. We reached that point because of a huge obstacle I faced in graduating. I had recently changed the focus of my studies when Northern Michigan introduced a new bachelor of science in urban planning.

The change of major forced me into higher-level math classes, such as trigonometry. I also had to take a course in public speaking. That class scared me more than the 400-level remote sensing and mapping classes I had to take.

Because urban planning involved interacting with elected officials, civil servants, and government organizations, it wasn't enough for us to know our stuff. We had to demonstrate our knowledge in public—hence the required end-of-year planning project we presented in front of the entire class. That one project made up sixty percent of our grade. The prospect of giving a presentation left me in a cold sweat—literally. I hated the idea of having to stand in front of other people and talk; it made me feel sick to my stomach. I shuddered just thinking about it.

On the day of the presentation, I watched the other students speak, my sense of dread rising. Finally it was my turn. I took a deep breath and stood. Telling myself to get it together, I tried to talk but my mind went blank. I froze. The words wouldn't come out of my mouth.

Time seemed to stand still. My mouth became dry. I felt dizzy. Dr. Joyle, my professor, asked me if I needed to pause and get some water. I nodded and stumbled out to the hallway. Finding a drinking fountain, I splashed my face with water and stared into the silver basin. *Pull yourself together, Brig!*

Back in front of the class, I took a deep breath and started again, but my delivery was no good. The words wouldn't come. "I can't do it," I conceded, before gathering my papers in frustration and walking out.

In his office later, Dr. Joyle lit his pipe before confirming the worst-case scenario. "You know that means you got an F for the whole class, right?"

I nodded gloomily. "I just don't like public speaking."

"Well, that's tough," he said. "You're just going to have to get over it. I'm going to give you a D, and you're going to have to repeat the class next year—and take a speech class to help you."

The next semester, Fran was accepting and affirming while I practiced my speeches for the public speaking class. She put up with my frustrations and meltdowns, offering encouragement, feedback, and sometimes laughter at just the right times. Although still not enjoyable, public speaking got easier. I found I could at least get through a presentation without freezing up, passing out, or stomping off. I ended up getting a B+ in speech class that following year, which felt to me like winning a gold medal.

By the time Christmas of our senior year came, Fran and I had been dating for over a year. One evening she came over to the house while I was watching a rerun of the old *Rudolph the Red-nosed Reindeer* special on TV with the guys. She took me into my bedroom and stunned me with the news that she was pregnant. It was almost surreal. I could hear Yukon Cornelius fighting off the abominable snowman in the other room as Fran's words shook me into adulthood. The thought of running or finding a way out didn't cross my mind. Before I could speak, Fran filled the void.

"I want you to know one thing," she told me. "I am having this baby, no matter what. I know some people are probably going to talk to me about not having it, but I am having this baby."

Life turns on moments like this.

Fran and I had gone to church together a few times. I did it as a goodwill gesture because I knew it was important to her. However, I didn't have any kind of faith background at all, and I wasn't completely sure about hers either. I didn't really know what I thought about the sanctity of life. I did not come out and suggest abortion to Fran, but if she had said that she wanted to get one, I am sure I would have offered her a ride to the clinic.

As it was, the resolute tone in her voice hit me hard. The next words out of my mouth were, "Let's get married."

"Brig, you don't have to marry me," she said. "I'll be okay. I know that everything will work out." I had seen how she was putting herself through school. When she said she would be okay, I knew it was true. But I found myself pleading for her to marry me.

Something about her sincerity and confidence touched me deeply. Here we were facing a major crossroad as young people, and she was giving me my freedom. It made me love her even more, and I felt something else stirring in me. I would never have planned my future this way, but being thrust into a sudden position of responsibility awakened a sense of excitement and anticipation.

At the same time, it became clear there was a fault line developing between my commitment to my rugby buddies and my future as a husband and father. Like the huddles I had been part of when I was younger—whether it was my pre-college friends, work friends, or sports teams—the rugby club had played an important part in my life. It had given me a vital sense of belonging and family, even an identity. But there came a point when I realized I needed to break away and find myself in a new, lifelong relationship.

If getting married meant saying goodbye to my rugby club brothers, then I was going to do it in style. Several of my teammates were in our tuxedo-clad wedding party, including my brother, Jon, my best man. Fran didn't know it, but I wore a pair of my green and gold rugby socks under my suit pants.

In all the years since, through our hard times and our triumphs, Fran has been the quiet strength behind everything I have achieved. If loving someone is like a voyage, Fran has navigated her share of rough water. In all our different seasons, she has been my encourager, enforcer, coach, confidant, assistant, and adviser. She has offered a soft shoulder and a firm hand just when it was needed. We're a team, and I couldn't ask for a better teammate.

CHAPTER FIVE

Broke, Not Poor

OUR IDENTITY SHOULD never get wrapped up in our current situation—especially if we're going through something difficult or painful. Difficulties should be viewed as challenges to overcome rather than conditions to accept.

I remember being nine years old and riding unbuckled in the front seat of my dad's Ford Galaxie 500. We were headed home after picking up rent money from a tenant who lived in one of the six small rental houses my parents owned. I was still numb from what I had just witnessed. My parents had cleaned up and freshly painted this property before the family moved in. It was not intended to be someone's "forever home," but it was a solid house located on a sidewalk-lined neighborhood street in downtown Lansing.

My dad and I stood just inside the front door as the man searched the house for an envelope of cash. My eyes adjusted to the only light in the room, a bluish glow from the TV.

I could make out at least six people in the room, and most were children my age or younger. I could see movement on the walls and the floor. I waited for my eyes to adjust more to figure out what I was seeing.

About that time the man came back into the family room and flicked on the lights to discover the envelope on the coffee table.

To my shock, I saw hundreds of cockroaches climbing the walls. They appeared and disappeared through the seams of the paneling like a grisly magic trick. They were crawling on the floor and even on the children watching TV, who didn't seem to care in the least.

As a kid, I was a worrier. I struggled in school, battled self-esteem issues, and had to deal with that horrible stutter. While driving home that day, I tried to form the sentence and practice it in my head, hoping it would come out right. I could see the frustration on my dad's face as the words spilled out of my mouth like rubber balls. What I finally got out was, "Dad, when I grow up, am I going to be like that?" His one-word answer was, "No."

As I grew up, the stuttering ended but not the fear of being poor. It didn't haunt my every waking moment but it would rear its ugly head on occasion like a recurring nightmare. Once a middle school math teacher was handing out our graded tests. When he dropped mine on the desk, it had so much red ink on it you would have thought someone had used it to gut a fish. He said, "I just cannot see how you will pass any math classes in high school." Cue the nightmare! My fear of failure and poverty created more triggers than a migraine headache.

Making the decision to marry Fran gave me a new sense of purpose and direction for my life.

Here was something for me to commit to, something to work for. Something to live for. Looking back, I believe that marrying Fran and having the baby was God's plan to redirect my life. On the surface—at least at that time in my life—it would have made more sense to abort the baby and hit a restart button.

Some may read this and feel that God is not going to bless a sinner. After all, Fran and I had premarital sex. Isn't that a sin? Yes, it is a sin. But in the constant currents under the surface of our day-to-day world, there is a battle of good and evil taking place. There are moving parts in our lives—a chess game, if you will, between these two opposites. The reality is, most of us are not capable of playing a basic game of checkers when it comes to life. But in the life of each person, good and evil are playing a one-hundred-layer game of chess every day.

For example, *Fran and I start dating and make each other better*: good. *Fran and I take the physical relationship too far, too fast*: bad. *We choose life over our personal freedoms*: good. Layers are added as the game plays on.

God will make the most out of our mistakes if we allow Him to work on us. Paul wrote, "And we know that for those who love God all things work together for good, for those who are called according to his purpose" (Romans 8:28 ESV). It doesn't mean

73

that everything is good—but God can bring good even out of the bad if we will let Him. When broken bones heal, the healed area becomes the strongest part of the bone. When a maple tree is distressed for lack of water and nutrients, it leaves markings in the grain called birds-eye. Bird's-eye maple is highly sought after for hardwood flooring and furniture.

In the same way, our troubles and mistakes often lead to new strength, increased character, and more resilience. Fran and I paid a dear price for our decision to have sex before marriage. There was a personal cost to accepting the responsibility, keeping the baby, and getting married. But overall, that string of decisions led to a lot of good. So goes the push and pull of good and evil fighting over our souls.

After a short engagement, Fran and I got married at St. Peter Cathedral in Marquette, Michigan. We had a one-night honeymoon at the Ramada Inn before returning to school for finals. My last exam was the day before graduation. I took part in the ceremony not knowing if I had enough credits to graduate. Fran and I posed together for photos in our gowns, hers draped over a growing belly.

Cue the poverty nightmare again! We had no health insurance and we were still in school. When I met with a man from the Department of Social Services, he treated me like human garbage. After I filled out the paperwork, he pulled out an envelope containing six crisp, never-folded twenty dollar bills and handed it to me.

"What's this?" I asked.

"What do you think it is? Take it and buy some food," he snapped.

"I'm not taking that," I said, sliding it back.

He slid it back. "Take it! Your wife and that baby need nutrition."

I slowly put the envelope in my pocket and walked out of the building in a stupor. I felt poor. I was on the slippery slope to poverty, and I wondered if there were a cockroach-infested house somewhere in my future.

As it turned out, I did have enough credits to receive my degree. But after graduation in 1986, jobs were hard to come by, especially for someone with a degree in urban planning and land use regulation. Fran and I moved to lower Michigan and rented an apartment in Haslett, a small town near where I grew up. After my own childcare experiences, we decided she would stay home with our baby.

I would do all I could to make ends meet.

I worked three part-time jobs loading trucks at the Meijer grocery store warehouse, loading beer trucks at Spartan Distributing, and moving furniture for Mom's Two Men and a Truck business (she had a couple of trucks at that time). Working all those jobs, I went from one hundred and seventy pounds at graduation to a hundred and forty by the next fall.

I finally landed a job as a warehouse manager for the beer distribution company. The pay was horrible but the job provided health insurance. I felt like my big toe had just touched the bottom of the pool in the deep end. The only direction was up.

That's when it dawned on me: *I'm not poor—I'm just broke!*

Being broke is just a point in time, but being poor is a state of mind. What did they have in common? *No money.* What separated them? Being poor, to me, meant being without hope. But I had hope. I had dreams. I had it in my heart to make something for myself and my family. This inspired me as Fran and I struggled through our twenties.

A year and a half later, we moved back to the Upper Peninsula. We bought a house in Ishpeming, a small mining town. The house had been abandoned for many years until a couple bought it but then gave up on it. I had my father-in-law, Bud, walk through the old house with me before Fran and I made the purchase.

Bud was a World War II veteran, a father of fourteen kids, and had held every job you can think of, from Chicago taxi driver to trapeze artist. He was short, stocky, and didn't talk much.

He stepped out of his car wearing navy blue Dickies work pants, a navy blue Dickies button-down work shirt, and a navy blue baseball hat. His white hair protruded from the back of his hat and contrasted with his brown leathery neck. He wore black work shoes and white socks.

You didn't mess with Bud. Bud walked through the house banging pipes and slamming doors.

He looked at me, announced, "This house will be here long after we're gone," and then walked out.

That was all I needed. The following week, Fran and I signed the papers on a ten-year balloon loan for $15,000. The house was ours. I drove right over and walked in. There was a January thaw and as the snow began to melt on the roof, it started raining *inside* the house. My jaw dropped as I looked around at this piece of hell we had just purchased. I sat on the floor and cried.

A week later, we moved in. Fran's mom and dad met us at the house. Bud looked around and barked, "Why did you buy this piece of shit?"

I was flabbergasted and felt dizzy. "Because you told me it would be here *long* after you and I died!"

"I did?" he asked.

"*Yes*, you did!" I said, hyperventilating.

"Oh. Well, I better go get my tools." Bud nailed me good. There is no humor better than Bud humor.

The old kitchen stove died after the first month. Bud said he had a stove for us and would bring it over. He came in with two boxes. Inside was a turquoise burner plate and a tiny oven.

"Bud, this isn't a stove."

"Nope, it's a burner plate and an oven for a fifth-wheel camper."

"What do we do with those?" I asked in shock.

Bud asked if I still had the old dresser that came with the house. "Yes, it's in the basement," I answered.

"Let's go get it," he replied.

He took a Sawzall and cut the top out of the dresser. Then he dropped the burner into the hole he just cut. He pulled the drawers out, cut a few spots, and slid the oven into the dresser drawer slots. He plugged it in.

Everything worked. He walked out and drove home.

F**k, maybe I'm poor after all, I thought. It was hideous, but it worked. We got so used to it that we didn't replace it for three years.

As the snow began to melt, I discovered to my horror that the yard was loaded with junk. Despite all the happenings that were out of my control, *this* was something I could control. I loaded my truck and with the only ten dollars cash I had in my wallet, I went to the dump. I asked the man who ran the dump what it would cost to dump my trash. "If you live in town, it's free," he said. Music to my ears!

"Sir, my name is Brig," I said. "I think we are going to become really good friends."

Anything that was not nailed down went to the dump. We didn't have two nickels to rub together when we bought that house, but as Fran's mom once said, "Soap is cheap!" The point being—poor people continue to live in squalor, but broke people keep pounding the rock to take what little they can control and do the most with it.

It was a long process with this house, but we were making improvements. A new roof, then new windows, doors, and siding. I bought an old wood boiler that Bud helped me install. We heated the house in winter with firewood that I spent all summer cutting, splitting, and stacking.

Things were coming together, but we still had our ongoing setbacks. Several years after moving in, I came downstairs and the first thing I spotted was a squirrel looking through the window. The only problem was that he was *inside* the house looking *out* the window! I looked to my left and our hundred-and-five-pound German shepherd/golden retriever mix, Quarters, was looking at the squirrel too. *Oh shit, this is going down,* I thought. The squirrel jumped down from the sill and ran past me.

Brycen, our one-year-old son, was standing between the kitchen and family room in a diaper. The squirrel ran between his legs. Quarters blew right through my son, sending him deep into the living room. In the chaos of a crying baby and lamps being smashed, the dog never caught the squirrel. I had a hard time sleeping that night. *Where is that damn squirrel? And, oh yeah, we still live in what is basically a glorified tree house.*

At the time of the squirrel incident, Fran and I had three kids and really were moving forward. We just started so far in a hole that it took a while to get out. Before the siding and windows went in, the house looked like an abandoned drug house. We later found out that the house's framing was made from old billboard lumber that some enterprising individual had repurposed.

I had friends who came to visit. I found out later some of them went home and told everyone how Fran and I were poor and living in a shack. We had another group stay with us for a weekend in the winter. I overheard them talking about the house as I was bringing wood to the boiler. "Could you imagine living in this shithole? Look at it."

This went on and on. I smiled to myself as I began feeding wood into the boiler. If I were poor, this would have shattered me. But I was only broke. The comments were painful to hear, but I knew we were moving in the right direction.

One morning as Fran and I were lying in bed, I said, "Fran, if we ever get a divorce, we will have to lawyer-up to see who *has to keep* this house." We laughed.

I went on. "Fran, look at us. We look like hobos! None of our sheets match. Not one pillowcase matches. It's like we are wrapped in clown's clothes!"

We just lay there laughing. It had been like that for years. The next week, we had matching sheets. A month later, matching towels. It may seem like small potatoes, but these were the step-by-step changes for a broke family moving forward. We saw ourselves as we were—pounders and grinders. We were broke, but we were *never* poor.

Whatever you're going through—whether it is family problems, marital struggles, or business challenges—you have a choice. You can shrug your shoulders and say, "This is just the way it is." Or you can face the difficult situation and look for ways to make improvements.

Start by asking, "What can I do to make this situation better?"

Abortion was not an option for Fran and me. But being unmarried and pregnant was not a good option either. So we did what we could.

Stuttering, freezing in front of the class, and failing school were difficult and painful experiences. It might have been easy for me to decide that I had a public speaking problem and then resolve myself to a different path in life. But that wasn't a good option. There were ways I could work to improve my situation.

It was the same with our job and living conditions, and it will be the same with many situations you face in life. You may have to look for a while, but you can almost always find ways to improve your circumstances. Focus on what you can control, and then take one step at a time.

With the responsibility of providing for a growing family, I was ready to start using my mind more than my back. I found a job selling insurance. Going from loading trucks to selling insurance was a huge leap, and working for a large insurance company had its own learning curve.

I had rate books for life, health, auto, and home-owner insurance, to name a few. People were no longer calling me to request my moving services—I had to initiate calls to people to get their business. It was tough.

Once I had that down, I found myself face-to-face with the customer. What I learned about people from my previous jobs came into play: Find a need and match it with a solution. Know when to talk and when to remain silent. Some people wanted detail, and others would get lost in it.

I also learned never to assume anything. I had people who lived in glorified shacks pay hundreds of dollars in cash for their first insurance premium. I also met people living in massive homes with beautiful cars in the driveways living hand to mouth without a dime to spare.

Our biggest tippers while working on the trucks were typically hardworking, blue-collar types who knew something about putting their backs into their work. These examples didn't always hold, but they taught me never to judge anyone by outward appearances.

James 2:3–4 says, "If you show special attention to the man wearing fine clothes and say, 'Here's a good seat for you,' but say to the poor man, 'You stand there' or 'Sit on the floor by my feet,' have you not discriminated among yourselves and become judges with evil thoughts?" (NIV).

No matter where you work or what you do, there are opportunities to learn new things you can use for the rest of your life.

Selling insurance provided a nice living to raise my family, but it wasn't my passion. I remembered how much I enjoyed moving—the freedom from a desk, the physical effort, and the challenge of every job being a little bit different. The satisfaction of helping people during a stressful time in their life, and seeing how Two Men and a Truck was expanding, began to stir something in me.

Mom was growing the brand through the franchise model. As more inquiries came in from potential franchisees, some of them wanted to talk to me to glean what I had learned from our early days. Melanie, my sister who was assisting my mom with running the business, asked me to help. I was happy to pass along anything that might be of benefit.

While helping a fellow insurance agent with his move, I began reminiscing about the good old days with Jon and friends. We talked about how much Two Men and a Truck had grown.

"Why don't you start a franchise?" asked one of the agents.

"Oh, I couldn't do that," I said. "I already have this job."

"Brig," he said, "you should go for it. Sometimes we have to take a risk in life. You know the business, and you love it. I can hear it in your voice. Don't worry about all the other stuff—that will work itself out. You should start that business."

To hear my friend just come out and say that was shocking, but it brought clarity. His statement lit a fire in me that had been waiting to be ignited. Fran and I talked it over and decided that, yes, we wanted to start a Two Men and a Truck franchise of our own. We finally did it, following the same path as my brother and sister. The year was 1991.

We discussed opening a franchise in Minneapolis, but at the time moving regulations in that state made it all but impossible to become licensed. Fran and I decided we would do better in Marquette, Michigan, even though it was a much smaller market. It started as a bare-bones, part-time thing. We added a second phone line to our house, and Fran used her customer service experience to book the jobs. The biggest expense we had was the loan for a truck, a Ford F600, which cost $25,000. That was $10,000 more than we had paid for our house!

Jon drove me down to Goshen, Indiana, to get the truck. Heading back on a beautiful spring day with the windows rolled down and the new vehicle aroma permeating the cab, I felt like I was on top of the world. Tom Petty came on the radio singing, "You can stand me up at the gates of hell, but I won't back down." I sang along at the top of my lungs.

Word of our business venture got back to my district insurance manager, a difficult guy to work under. To his credit, he was very successful, but he had no idea how to motivate his team. He bullied and belittled people, calling them out in public if they had not performed well.

I accompanied him on sales calls where he could be a little warmer, but he would sometimes get into political arguments with clients. I'd sit nearby feeling awkward and vow to myself that I would never treat people that way.

Learning from our leaders can be a double-edged sword. It dawned on me that we can learn to be great from great leadership, but we can also be taught just as much by poor leadership. I think it's helpful to take these moments and turn them into an exercise—think of a bad experience and what could have been done or said that would have produced a better outcome.

When my manager became aware of our Two Men and a Truck franchise, he wasn't happy. He made it clear he would be watching to make sure I wasn't doing any moving work on his time. He had every right to make his point, but his attitude was just another example of the negativity I wanted to escape.

We started low-key. Fran did most of the work, handling the calls and booking the jobs. I would interview prospective movers and pitch in on the weekends when I was free. Little by little, business picked up as word got out. It helped that our Two Men and a Truck vehicle was parked on a self-storage lot on the main highway between Marquette and Negaunee. We had free advertising to thousands of motorists who passed by each day.

By the time our third and last child arrived, I knew it was time to make a clean break from the insurance company. I went to my district manager to tell him I was leaving. Trying to make things a little easier for him, I decided to give three weeks' notice instead of the typical two. He looked up from signing a pile of checks.

"So, what are you going to do?"

"I'm going to run our moving business," I said.

"Ha," he said dismissively. "Good luck." And he went back to signing his checks. No handshake. No goodbye. Nothing.

I smiled in disbelief as I walked out of his office. From there, I headed to the office of Jim Moore. Jim was a big, older man who reminded me of John Wayne. After retiring as a Michigan state trooper, he began selling insurance. Jim was a natural and had been promoted to branch manager.

People loved Jim. When he became my boss, he asked me to set up appointments that we would run together. He had a booming laugh, and he laughed a lot during our meetings. First, he would find common ground with clients. Then, after a bit of chit-chat, he would get to business. In almost all cases, we would have someone insured when we left. Jim added two years to my career by changing my attitude. He made the job fun and enjoyable.

As I walked into his office, Jim looked up at me from his desk. He had a pair of small, thin-wired reading glasses balanced on the end of his nose. I told him I was giving my three-week notice, and he stared intently as he snapped the glasses off his nose. I thought, *Oh shit, here we go.*

After what felt like ten seconds, Jim said, "Can I come with you?" It was one of the kindest, most grace-filled things anyone had ever said to me. Jim was full of encouragement. I left his office feeling more than whole.

Twenty years later, Jim called. I told him he was the best boss I ever had. In his classic booming laugh he said, "Oh, Brig, I was a lousy manager."

I responded, "From you, Jim, I learned there is a lot of room for grace when you're a boss. I learned to laugh more too."

Jim laughed hard and said, "Well, I sure am glad I made this call."

Fran and I knew we had to run things lean if we were going to make it. She took a teaching position at a school that gave us benefits, and she taught a night class once a week. With me now working from home, we were able to avoid putting the kids in full-time daycare.

We still weren't making a fortune, but I could see progress and potential. Equally important, my spirits were much lighter. I felt like I was the master of my destiny, not the servant of someone else's. I loved the variety in our work, never knowing what kind of people or job might come next.

CHAPTER SIX

Going All In

AFTER GETTING OUR Two Men and a Truck franchise up and running, there were a few times we almost reached our limit. Days would go by without a call. I would occasionally dial our business phone just to see if it was working.

One time we made a five-hour move in a snowstorm and received payment for $262. We were cold and exhausted. When we finished, we picked up a tire that was being repaired for one of our trucks. The bill came to—$262. Besides using it as an example to explain to my employees where "all the money goes," that was a tough one to swallow.

I had always known that the moving business is seasonal. Summer is the busiest time—it's when families relocate between their children's school years. This seasonal tendency is intensified in places where the winters are harsh, such as Michigan's Upper Peninsula. People do all they can to avoid moving in subzero temperatures with snow piled high.

So, most people want to move in the same tight summer window. We called this the "smelt run." Smelt are tiny freshwater fish in the Great Lakes. For a couple of weeks in the spring, when the conditions are just right, they will run up small rivers and creek tributaries to spawn. When this happens, their numbers are so thick you can almost walk across them.

Our moving followed the rhythm of nature in Michigan's Upper Peninsula—it went into deep hibernation in the winter. For days at a time, the truck would look like a lump under a heavy blanket of snow, just another part of the desolate landscape. Learning and rolling with the rhythms of the market was necessary for survival, but so was diversifying.

We got a call one day from the owner of a high-end boutique furniture store in Marquette. Their old delivery truck broke down, and they were in a panic. They needed someone to deliver one of their expensive custom couches. We were there instantly.

When expanding a business, it's important to showcase that you are fit for the task at hand. You are proving yourself not only to the customer but also to your employees and, quite honestly, to yourself. Stepping into the unknown, you need to know you're up to the challenge.

For us, taking on a couple of high-end jobs was a big step for our little business. Can we deliver a ten-thousand-dollar couch? *Hell yes, we can!*

I knew we had moved heavier, secondhand sleeper sofas to deer camps in North Ishpeming. Our issue now was to make sure we presented our company well for this new level of clientele.

We stepped back and asked ourselves: *What could we control? People's perception of us.*

Our guys looked athletic and sharp in their crisp matching uniforms and their sparkling clean truck. Pads were neatly folded, stacked, and strapped down. Our dollies and equipment were stowed away in perfect order. Our paperwork was neat, orderly, and easy to understand. We gave solid handshakes, made eye contact, and offered smiles with every move.

Our confidence radiated like the warmth of a crackling fire on a wintry Michigan night. We arrived and parked next to the furniture store owner's old rusty truck. By the time we walked out of there, we had made a solid impression. The furniture store owner trusted we would treat her valuable merchandise well. She had confidence that her client's delivery would be smooth and professional.

The delivery was to a high-end neighborhood we had never been in professionally. That meant it was time to make another lasting impression, this time on our customer's client. With a proper introduction, handshake, and smile, we got to work. We even added doorjamb protectors to protect their front door as we delivered the flowery couch. We were very happy to move furniture around this beautiful living room until the homeowner was satisfied that she'd found the perfect spot for her new piece.

In some ways it felt like we had made the big

leagues. We were ready to step into a new arena of larger homes and designer furniture. Mom's words came back to me from years before, when I was just a kid running in from the barn. *Run with purpose.*

We ran with purpose, and we nailed our first high-end move. We left with a hearty handshake and received a nice tip—much nicer that what we expected from a single couch delivery.

Soon the boutique furniture store was using our little company to do all their deliveries. We also cleaned and organized their entire warehouse. Our truck was now seen at Marquette's most influential homes and apartments—not just delivering single pieces but making full household moves.

During this time of business growth, I was asked to market Two Men and a Truck's franchise opportunities. I worked on the trucks during the day and made phone calls in the evening. Once we went through the franchise awarding process, qualified prospects would come for a visit. I would drive down and give them a tour of our small corporate office as well as the Lansing franchise.

The time from the first call to signing the franchise agreement could be anywhere from three to eight months. I drew on my experience of being a mover, especially how I had learned to read customers and take care of their needs. It was a tool I had sharpened as a successful insurance agent, protecting people's property, lives, wages, and retirement.

In my new role as franchise developer, I was offering people a new way of life. The transition was a fluid one. I was comfortable in my new role, and it taught me an important lesson: never sleepwalk during your career.

We all have a tool bag, and it is our job to fill that bag with our talents and experiences. These tools, old and new, can be utilized to move up or even cross over into a new profession.

King David in the Old Testament was a great example of someone who made use of his tool bag. David was the youngest and smallest of seven brothers. He was the runt. However, he was anointed king of Israel, chosen over all his brothers who seemed more qualified. David began as a shepherd boy, not exactly an apprenticeship for becoming king.

But in God's plan, that's precisely what it was.

God developed David's skills and talents during his day-to-day life of being a shepherd. One of those skills was to become lethal with a slingshot. David used this ability to protect the sheep in his flock. He learned to take out lions and bears. He later made a name for himself when he pulled out his slingshot and buried a rock deep into the skull of a nine-foot armored giant named Goliath.

David had no warrior training on his resume—he just dipped into his tool bag.

As individuals, we must continue to learn and grow through the experiences and challenges we face. When you become a leader, you are looking for modern-day Davids to bring up and nurture. They come in all shapes, colors, and sizes, male and female. (Here I go again with my salty language—I call them *ass-kickers*.)

We weren't just looking for guys with muscles. We needed smart people who had strong communication skills and could think on their feet—a guy like Aaron Riutta.

A gangly teenager, he was part of a large family who lived nearby in Ishpeming. Aaron delivered our newspaper when he was young—a modern-day shepherd boy.

He saw me splitting wood in the yard one morning, something I loved to do, and asked if I would pay him to do it for me. I told him no thanks, but that didn't discourage Aaron. He asked again a few days later. He was becoming an annoyance—so much so that I tried to make sure I was not outside when he delivered the paper. At the same time, I admired his enthusiasm. You just don't see kids his age hustling for cash. It made me think back to the days when I raked leaves.

When Aaron was sixteen, he learned Fran and I were the owners of the Two Men and a Truck vehicle he saw around town. He begged me for a job. I sensed Aaron had the attitude I was looking for, but

I wasn't sure he could handle the workload—he was a stringy kid.

I told him that I'd take him on when he could bench press two hundred pounds. He was so excited. He'd give me progress reports along with my newspaper.

"Hey, Brig, one forty," he'd say.

"Brig, one forty-five."

"Brig, one fifty."

One Sunday afternoon, I was sitting on the couch at home watching TV with the kids when I got a call from the local gym. There was the clanking of metal in the background and then Aaron's voice, a little breathless.

"I got it, Brig," he said. "Two hundred pounds."

"That's great, Aaron," I told him. "Congratulations. But I have to see it. Think you can do it again?"

I grabbed my coat and drove to the gym. There, surrounded by his high school friends, Aaron locked out a wobbly two-hundred-pound bench press. I high-fived him and told him I would handpick a move for us to work together.

A two-bedroom apartment move came up a few weeks later, and I knew the two of us could handle it. As we emptied one of the rooms, the remaining items came into focus—a couple of old headstones, each weighing about ninety pounds.

Aaron squatted to pick one up. "Hey, Brig, do you

typically move these?" Aaron asked in his thick Finnish Yooper accent.

"Nope, this is a first for me," I said.

I told Aaron this job would never stop surprising him with the things people cherish. Aaron moved both headstones with no trouble at all. Having passed his mover's test with flying colors, he became a stalwart Two Men and a Truck team member.

He would later do his high school internship with us, helping man the office in addition to working on the trucks. Aaron was the poster boy for capitalizing on opportunities. He took every responsibility he could and became an example of how to climb within our small company. After finishing school, Aaron moved to Arizona where he opened a Two Men and a Truck franchise before becoming an investment banker.

In a video our corporate office made on our past front line employees' lessons learned, Aaron fondly recalled his time at Two Men and a Truck, citing those experiences as formative for what he later achieved.

"There is a big difference between moving furniture and being an investment banker," he reflected. "But a lot of the foundations of what I do now I learned while working with Two Men and a Truck: good customer service, treating people as though they are always right, and learning the challenges that go with all types of jobs."

Aaron's comments resonate with others who come

to Two Men and a Truck. They are learning not just the moving business but also, skills to apply no matter where life takes them. Aaron went all in, and it helped him for years to come.

At this point, Fran and I were finally starting to gain traction in our business and financial lives.

Fran was teaching full-time while I was bringing in commissions earned for awarding new franchises. With this and our Marquette operation's growth, we were able to expand to two trucks.

We continued to renovate our once-abandoned house—the one we bought for $15,000—into a warm place we now called home. It reminded me a bit of the old Granville house in *It's a Wonderful Life*, one of my all-time favorite movies. Like George and Mary Bailey, Fran and I took a rundown property and somehow turned it into a home. While it still had its "oh, my God" moments, we had created many fond memories.

Still, we came to a place where we wanted and needed to expand for our growing family. After some discussion, Fran and I decided we'd like to design and build our next home. We began looking for available lots in the Ishpeming area. We were growing roots in this tight-knit community, and we could envision our upward mobility there.

Meanwhile, our business was ripe for growth. Our name was out. Phone calls to make household moves were coming in from sixty to one hundred miles away.

We opened a satellite office in Escanaba. We were considering another in Iron Mountain with the possibility of adding storage.

With one phone call, however, the game changed.

My sister, Melanie, called and asked if we would move back to Lansing. She and Mom had become involved with the International Franchise Association (IFA) and had learned a lot about effective franchising. They realized Two Men and a Truck needed an on-site person to manage franchise development.

I told Melanie how Fran and I had built a nice life up north. Melanie said she understood if we decided to stay, but she would have to hire a full-time franchise development person in-house either way. For me, this sounded more like a train whistle leaving the station than it did a job offer. Given the struggles we'd faced during our years in the Upper Peninsula of Michigan, this invitation should have seemed like an easy one. It wasn't.

I knew how much Fran liked being close to her family. She had secured a good job teaching at the local high school. We had made very close friends, and we'd grown quite fond of the area. But as I thought about it, I realized that this home office position was too good an opportunity to pass up. I sensed that Two Men and a Truck was on the cusp of going really big, and I wanted to be part of making that happen.

Fran didn't feel the same. It took a lot of time and

effort to build a tapestry of friends and support for our kids—people such as doctors, teachers, and childcare. She didn't want to move farther from her family.

Her response took the wind out of my sails. Her points were valid, yet I could not shake the feeling that this was something we had to do. We tried to talk through this huge all in moment, but our conversations would end in a stalemate with both of us frustrated and exhausted.

Another sticking point was the success in our lives. Look where we were. Look where we wanted to go. Wasn't it good enough?

This was not only one of Fran's points but one of mine as well, deep in my mind. One night when Fran went to bed, I stayed downstairs and mulled it over again. I pulled out a piece of paper and a pen and wrote her a letter. In that letter, I poured out my heart.

I told Fran I knew it must be hard for her to think about moving farther away from her extended family again but that we needed to think about our family. I acknowledged that it was safe and convenient in Ishpeming. We lived in a small community where people all knew one another and didn't lock their doors, but that didn't represent the bigger world. One day, the kids would grow up and move out into that bigger world. Living in a more diverse area would allow our kids to experience more and present more opportunities for them.

I recounted all the risks and struggles we had come through together. All the times I'd felt I was dying at my dead-end insurance sales desk, with no real hope. We had built our lives with all-in moments—this was not new to us. We had been through a lot: becoming pregnant, getting married, moving and fixing up this once-abandoned house, and starting this little moving company.

I explained how proud I was that we carved a living out of a population made up of very independent, we-can-do-it-ourselves people and how we took the opportunities in front of us.

I told her I needed to tell Melanie *yes*. This move was our next step—our biggest step because it would affect all five of us. This was a once-in-a-lifetime opportunity for all of us. If we missed this, I would view it as a failure on my part to be the best I could for my family.

I poured it all out, ending with some statements that I knew could be viewed as drawing a line in the sand: *I am deciding to do this for the betterment of all of us. You have to decide for yourself, Fran. I'm going, and I hope you come with me. Love, Brig.*

The next morning before I left on an early moving job, I placed the letter on the table for Fran to find. When I returned that evening, there was a written reply from her in the same place. In her letter, she told me that she and the kids were coming. She loved me and believed in me. Her response brought tears to my eyes.

We moved a few months later.

Getting Fran on board was a huge relief. I wasn't trying to be a jerk by pressing hard, but I had a bone-deep conviction that the move was the right thing to do. It would be nice to pretend that this confidence came from my growing personal faith, but that would be painting too simple a picture. I wasn't sure where the sureness came from—I just knew I had to act on it. Looking back, I would say God was moving despite my being unaware of His hand in it.

According to legend, Spanish conquistador Hernán Cortés took several sailboats, men, horses, and weapons to modern-day Mexico to overthrow the Aztec empire in the early 1500s. As they reached the shore, they found themselves staring down half a million Aztecs waiting on the beach. Cortés and his group tippy-toed back to the boats, put their tails firmly between their legs, and sailed back to Spain.

After giving it much thought, Cortés realized the problem and returned to Mexico. This time, when the men, horses, and supplies came to shore, Cortés ordered his men to burn all the boats. They pleaded with Cortés to change his mind. Cortés insisted, scuttling any opportunity to retreat. The only way to overthrow the Aztec empire was to fight. As the boats burned and sank to the bottom of the ocean, so did the opportunity to run.

MOVING FORWARD

As Fran and I loaded our moving trucks and pulled out of Ishpeming, I could hear the crackling fire and smell the smoke from our boats burning in the rearview mirror. Looking back on my life, my most significant moments of change came during times like these. *Burn the boats*.

CHAPTER SEVEN

The Learning Curve

PACKING UP EVERYTHING into two trucks and moving into a new home four hundred miles away was a good reminder of what our customers go through. It was also a reminder that the chaos doesn't end there—getting kids signed up for school, finding new doctors, a different church, hairstylists, grocery stores. The list goes on and on.

As days turned into weeks and then months, we settled into a new normal. Work life became easier now that Fran and I were no longer managing a franchise location. I immersed myself into franchise development, which I had been doing part-time up north. I also wore the hat of a franchise business consultant (FBC), helping franchisees with their day-to-day operational activities. I loved my job.

I didn't realize it at the time, but both roles shared the same foundation: trust. An existing franchisee needed to know they could trust me and that I would work for their good. They had to believe that my success came only from their success.

If you can't eat the food on your plate, do not add more. Translation: Don't add more franchise locations if you cannot service the ones you have. It's a mistake several franchise systems make. They fail to realize that the best tool to convert solid franchise leads is your existing franchisees. Again, trust is key.

Using our strong franchisee relationships, we were poised to add more locations. There were thousands of different franchising opportunities all claiming to be the best. This is where Two Men and a Truck held a huge advantage. Almost all our franchisees were happy and growing! Knowing this changed the way we communicated with prospective franchisees. We could confidently differentiate ourselves from most franchise concepts.

A prospective franchisee once came into my office and said, "So let me hear your spiel." I simply looked at him and said, "I don't have one." We stared at each other for several seconds before I continued.

"Not to sound condescending, but we don't need you," I said. "Our system is set up to allow our existing locations to add more trucks and get deeper into their markets. Our operations department is four times larger than our franchise development department. If you're a good fit, we would be better with you, but we don't need you."

I found that this set potential franchisees at ease knowing they would not be sold a bill of goods. I would later give them a list of existing locations to call and ask about their views of the Two Men and a Truck system. I would even provide them a list of individuals who were no longer with us to ask why they left. Transparency is essential.

Being transparent up front paid dividends down the road when setting expectations and trouble-shooting. There were several cases when we had to quell the excitement of new franchisees. Some became so excited about the conversations they had with our existing franchisees that they could hardly control themselves. A potential franchisee is likely to be very excited about this new chapter in their lives. Our job was not to feed this euphoria but to take off their rose-colored glasses and discuss any issues. Franchising, like all things in life, has a good side and a not-so-good side. When something is good, that does not mean it is perfect—it means the good outweighs the bad.

It may sound counterintuitive to tell prospective franchisees that they will become frustrated, even angry with the system at times, but this is how to build trust.

On occasion, I would ask, "Can you handle being a loser? What I mean is, can you deal with being on the losing end of a disagreement?"

There will be a time in the franchise system when they will be told no on a marketing or service idea that they want to try. In essence, the franchisee will not get their way—they will be the loser from time to time.

We'd also point out several cases where the franchisee would be a winner in our system. We'd typically get a lot of head nodding and understanding during this talk, but I knew they would call at some point down the line to discuss their frustrations. After listening, I would remind them about this discussion of being on a losing end of a disagreement and then affirm the many places were they are winning in our system. Those talks almost always ended in a civil way and with clearer understanding. We could move forward because of the transparency we shared from the beginning.

This method of incorporating trust and transparency applies in all aspects of life. One of the best examples is coaching Little League. Coaches will have issues with the parents' and players' expectations. It's important to deal with it up front.

I would send a letter to the parents of the players at the start of the season. *Our goal is that your child will have enough fun that they will want to play next year. The batting order is based on when players show up to the game. Some challenged players will only play positions that will protect them from hard-hit balls until we can build up their skills. A loud voice from me is coaching, not yelling, and is never meant to demean a player. If you are frustrated, please call me and don't scream from the bleachers.*

I would have the players sit in a semicircle around me and hand them each a grass-stained baseball from the last season. "Hold it to your nose and smell hard," I would say. "If you smelled an old baseball a hundred years ago, it would smell the same. Best smell in the world."

From there, I would let them know there's a good chance they would get hurt, but it would be worth it. Bloody noses and lips and even black eyes can happen. That has also happened over the last hundred years. "It will hurt, but you will be okay—it's part of the game. There are times when you will strike out, drop the ball, or let one go between your legs. Don't get upset. It is part of the game."

Trying to calm an infielder who just took a grounder to the nose is easier when they are reminded of the talk—and that they will be okay. Whether in Little League, relationships, or business, being up front with the risks and talking through them build trust. There is no need to sell at this point because the commitment has already been made. Continue to build trust and remain transparent.

One hand washes the other when it comes to collaboration and trust. I've found that leaders who lasted for the long haul gathered ideas and thoughts from several people affected by the challenge at hand. They adjusted their expectations accordingly. On the surface this may sound trite, but there are three very good reasons to do this.

First, you identify what you don't know. Leaders often do not have all the information needed to make the best management decision. *You don't know what you don't know.* By collaborating with coworkers, vendors, and customers, more information is collected. Actively listening and asking specific questions provides additional insight.

Second, going through this process allows you to build a team. The people who participated in step one are now invested. Go one step further and allow these trusted people to collect more information and make decisions that can affect the business. Invite them into the adventure and excitement of sharing the spoils of the fight.

Third, gathering information and ideas allow time to pass. While you are accumulating data and joining forces with others, the challenge defines itself—evolving and showing itself more clearly.

Give it enough time to be seen.

The best quarterbacks do not take a snap and immediately throw the ball. They take a couple of steps back and read the defense, allowing its coverage to be exposed. In the meantime, the linemen and receivers also make adjustments to neutralize and expose the defense. Plays can be won and lost by a good block, a different route from a receiver, or the quarterback's footwork. Yes, there are times when we get sacked. As a team, we must work together and adjust.

Like football, we will not win every play in business but this problem-solving system sets us up to win more than we lose. As I worked my way up in the industry, I used this system for simple and complex problems alike. The carpet in my office was well worn by people with issues—and ideas on how to solve them.

Without realizing it at the time, I employed this same leadership method with the Little League team I coached. I would take dads who normally sat in the bleachers to watch practice and involve them. Three of the dads became head coaches themselves. It gave me great satisfaction watching them coach.

One of the players had a very vocal mother—almost to the point of being obnoxious. I spoke with her after our first game and discovered she knew a lot about baseball. She knew how to keep the scorebook, so I asked if she would keep the book for us, and she did for the remainder of the season.

Another dad was good at making rotation schedules for our players. He would send those to me before every game. I would go through them and make any adjustments if needed. Another dad hit fly balls to the outfield while I hit grounders to the infield before each game.

Sharing all those responsibilities allowed me to work with the players who needed more instruction. It was now *our* team, not *my* team. When things went haywire—which they did from time to time—these parents had a different perspective than if they were only in the bleachers. I was also offered constructive feedback rather than "Monday morning quarterback" comments from people who were not invested.

This management style not only built teams and addressed problems—it also exposed leaders.

A gold prospector rolls water, rock, and sand back and forth in his tin pan. Occasionally, he may pull out of the mess a single gold nugget. This is no different from finding that one leader in the thick of tackling an issue. We found our CEO, president, CFO, HR executive, several multi-unit franchisees, and other exceptional leaders in the chaos of a challenge. They discovered what they were capable of and, in the process, found themselves and their worth.

The five years I spent at Northern Michigan University for my four-year degree had not prepared me for any of this. I learned a lot more from the pounding I took as a young husband and father, trying to make a home out of a once-abandoned house while scratching out a living as an insurance agent. Life is sometimes the best teacher.

I realized that the most valuable lessons I learned were not found in courses at school. Instead, the most impactful takeaways were discovered during the struggle to persevere while finding and maintaining hope. The importance of celebrating small wins was enough to keep me motivated as I continued to move forward.

During this time I could see I was changing. I was growing up. The years of nagging and worrying about being poor were in the rearview mirror. My experiences and struggles were more than just painful memories. When these experiences were mined and carefully considered, they became lessons learned. Many times, those lessons provided answers to current problems.

The fact that I didn't take a single business class in college did not stop me from growing a business. I knew every aspect of this business from the ground up, from being on the back end of a piano going upstairs to spearheading franchise development to being a franchise business consultant.

My skills of explaining a need and selling a solution were sharpened during my insurance days. Those skills would be used throughout my life. I remember delivering life insurance proceeds to a grieving mother whose only child died suddenly of heart failure at eleven years old. I sat with her as she cried.

She confided in me that she had only recently stopped going to the bus stop. For a while after he passed she continued to go see the kids get off. She held on to a glimmer of hope that her son might get off, too, and end her nightmare. She would then drive to the cemetery and stare at his gravestone. Returning home, she would go into his bedroom to smell his clothes so she would not forget what he smelled like.

I drove home in tears—this was the first time I had experienced what it felt like to lose a child. They don't teach you these things in college or during orientation at a new job. While working for years on the trucks, we watched life unfold before us daily. Many moves were sad—death, divorce, and moving the elderly to assisted living, just to name a few.

Putting the lessons I had learned into practice enabled me to gain traction. As the franchise developer, I was no longer selling life insurance policies—I was selling a whole new way of life by awarding franchise opportunities. As a franchise business consultant, I was no longer motivating just movers but business owners as well. I decided who received a franchise and had the final decision of who could lose a franchise through nonrenewal of a franchise agreement or termination. I did not take my responsibilities lightly.

Mostly, I was a motivator. I remembered my insurance manager, Jim Moore, who was upbeat, knowledgeable, and bigger-than-life with his booming laugh. Jim would also correct me, but the correction was easier to accept because I knew I was loved and respected.

I knew what it was like to be a have-not. Now I was established and doing well. As I mentioned previously, by this time in my life, I felt that I had finally arrived.

There was a satisfaction that carried over each time I drove home and pulled into our driveway in Tacoma Hills. Before making an offer on our house there, I had arranged for an inspector to go through the place. I didn't want to find it was made from old billboards like our once-abandoned house up in Ishpeming. The inspector looked around and confidently told me it was a rock.

"You could land a helicopter on that roof," he assured me. "How old are you?" he asked.

"Thirty-two years old," I said.

"Wow, thirty-two years old," he said, nodding in approval. His comment was the slamming of a door on my past struggles.

I was reflecting on the inspector's comment that day I pulled into the driveway, thinking it was just about time for my cigar and whiskey celebration.

Time to mow the lawn and clean the pool. If I find myself alone when my chores are done, it might be time to fire up that stogie and have that whiskey on ice.

I had made it.

CHAPTER EIGHT

Finding My Feet

A SENSE OF DESPONDENCY draped over me. A few days after my anticlimatic whiskey and cigar celebration, I no longer felt energized about the challenges ahead of me, which was something I had never experienced before. Sitting at my desk in the Two Men and a Truck office, I caught sight of a thought-provoking advertisement while scanning the news online. The ad read, *What in the world would happen if Jesus came back from Heaven and took all His followers during our lifetime?*

This is the life-changing moment I referred to at the end of chapter one. For some reason, the question intrigued me. I knew that He would take me with Him. After all, I went to church regularly, Fran and I gave money to good causes, and we prayed before dinner. Plus, I didn't hang out in bars and chase women—I was a dedicated family man. There was no question I'd get chosen.

In fact, I quietly considered myself to be probably one of His top picks, a five-star recruit. I interpreted the successes Fran and I were enjoying as evidence of His favor. Having found out that Fran was pregnant while we were two penniless college students, we'd done the right thing by marrying and keeping our unplanned baby. And we had worked hard. *Be good for God, and He will be good to you.* I was staying inside the lines.

But the scenario of Jesus's return stayed with me and, for a moment, I forgot the heaviness I'd felt. It hadn't entirely evaporated, but I sensed a measure of relief. I decided to order a copy of the advertised book, figuring that reading it might get me out of my funk.

Tim LaHaye and Jerry B. Jenkins's novel *Left Behind* arrived in the mail a few days later. The apocalyptic story grabbed my attention from the first chapter when passengers on a jet disappeared in midflight. They had been "raptured" like millions of other believers worldwide, taken into heaven to be with Jesus. It sounded crazy but compelling.

My initial confidence about being part of that group, if such a thing were really to happen, started to fade. Among those who didn't get taken up in the story—left instead to make their own way in a dangerous world—was a pastor! That stopped me in my tracks.

If a full-time religious guy didn't make the cut, where does that leave me? From the beginning, the book began to rattle my already shaky faith foundation. I welcomed the disturbance for the simple fact that it distracted me from how unsettled I had been feeling.

Some of the story's characters were in the Bible and were familiar to me. Other passages rang a bell from weekly services at St. Martha Parish in Okemos.

I decided to check out for myself the parts of the book that were new to me. I had to know how much of what I was reading was fiction and how much was real.

Though Fran and I attended church regularly, as did many in the Catholic circles we moved in, we didn't read the Bible ourselves. We left that to the priest to do on our behalf and then report back.

If you look hard enough in most Christian households, you will find a Bible somewhere in the house. I found one on our bookshelf and began navigating my way through, doing spot checks on the scriptures cited in *Left Behind*. The Bible started opening up to me as if I had discovered a secret room in our house that had been hidden for years.

I remembered a conversation with an employee who suggested that if I ever read the Bible, I should start with the book of John. He told me the Old Testament can be a bit heavy for new Bible readers. When we had that conversation, I reasoned that attending church once a week checked the box.

I had convinced myself that was more than what most people were doing.

But now, I was realizing that simply going to Mass once a week was equivalent to going to the gym, doing ten pushups, toweling off, and going home. The secret room I had found was captivating me. I could not peek in only to shut the door and leave. I had to walk in and explore.

Every morning, I'd go into the office half an hour early to read the Bible and would mull over what I had read throughout the day. I didn't really understand much about prayer, but I asked God to help me make sense of the Scriptures. At night in bed, I'd pick up *Left Behind*. Later I moved on to the other books in the series.

Fran couldn't help but notice my sudden fascination with religious questions, but she didn't push me. She could see that my mood was lightening bit by bit, so she gave me room to think and explore. One day we met at a bookstore café. As we ate, Fran mentioned that she had started listening to a preacher on the radio named Charles Stanley.

"He takes Bible readings and applies them to today's life. It's interesting," she said. "Interesting how the issues we have now were no different from what they were a few thousand years ago."

I tuned in on my way back to the office to catch the end of his daily broadcast. I wanted to chuckle at his Southern accent, which fit my image of the quintessential Baptist preacher, but I was struck by his words—warm, wise, and well-chosen. He spoke with a quiet certainty and authority, referring to the Bible in a simple, matter-of-fact way. Back in the Two Men and a Truck parking lot, I sat in my car to hear him finish before going back to work.

Lunchtime with Charles Stanley became a regular

habit. Stanley would mention things that I had just read in the Bible, bringing light and understanding to them. All the different things I was reading and hearing were like pieces of a jigsaw puzzle gradually snapping together. I was curious to see what the final picture would be.

A while back, a couple of guys who worked at the Two Men and a Truck corporate office asked me if they could start a Bible study during the lunch hour. I was noncommittal, and they had not pressed the issue. I went back to them and asked if they were still interested.

We started with a book by Max Lucado called *He Chose the Nails*. As with Charles Stanley, I had no idea who Max Lucado was. I was totally unaware of his status as a hugely popular pastor and author, but I loved how he told everyday stories from his own life. He also used modern-day parables as illustrations that matched events from the Bible, connecting the contemporary world with ancient writings. Between our weekly get-togethers at the office, I would occasionally ask one of the guys about a Bible question I had.

Something was happening inside me. There was more to life than waking up and being pushed and pulled by the random wind and currents of life. I couldn't put my finger on it, but a better way of living was coming into focus. I could feel it.

I wanted to chase it.

Over the course of several weeks I sensed my heart opening to a new possibility, like the way a flower opens to the sun's warming rays. It came down to a dawning realization: I did not have a true relationship with Jesus Christ.

I knew a bit about Jesus. I tried to do things I thought He would like, and I tried not to do things that would upset Him. But I didn't know Jesus personally, like the people in the *Left Behind* series. I didn't know Him the way Charles Stanley and Max Lucado talked about knowing Him.

Yes, I had been baptized and confirmed in the church. But now curiosity was driving me. My interest in God was about more than just qualifications for getting into heaven. I realized that my relationship with God wasn't about what I could earn. It wasn't about what God was asking *from* me.

Knowing God was all about what He was *gifting* me.

God revealed His love for me and His patience with me. In a nutshell, God showed me grace. I deserved a beatdown for the way I lived my life and wore my faith like a common piece of clothing.

After God had my attention, His resources poured into me like fresh water to a man dying of thirst. There was no anger or fear from a higher power who was done with me. Instead, I simply felt loved.

I had never been given this kind of love before. If someone had tried to give it to me, I must not have been able to accept it. Because of this, I had not been able to give that kind of love to others.

I still had a lot of questions, but I knew what I needed to do. At home one evening, I went to the basement and sat on the weight bench. It was the same place where several weeks prior I had been ambushed by tears, unable to lift the bar.

This now seemed the perfect place to say the truth—that I realized, in my strength and effort, I could not earn what I wanted and needed. Here was a weight I could not lift on my own no matter how hard I tried. This would be like no other prayer I had ever prayed.

My prayers up to this point drew a fine line between talking with God and a conversation with Santa Claus. I offered wish lists of things I needed, or problems—and even people—that I wanted to go away. The kind of prayer I was about to give exposed my heart, leaving me completely vulnerable. It felt like I was jumping into the unknown. If no one caught me, I would be severely hurt.

"God," I began timidly. "I'm not the sharpest tool in your spiritual shed, and I don't even know if I am doing this right. And this is just between You and me. Jesus, I want You to come into my life. I want You to be my Lord and Savior. I'm sorry for taking You for granted all these years, for thinking that I could earn Your love by what I did. We don't know each other very well—I mean, You know me, of course—but I want to know You more."

The significance of a turning point often isn't realized until we travel farther down the road. That was true for me in that moment. There was no heavenly choir or burst of light when I got up from the weight bench—just a quiet awareness of something settling inside me. I didn't sense God speaking to me, but I felt like He was probably smiling, and that was enough.

While I still had many questions, I knew something had been resolved once and for all in that simple encounter with God. I was confident that I wasn't going to be left behind anymore. More importantly, I felt this conversation had to happen to continue my pursuit of a new life.

I sensed that life was going to change, even if I was not sure how. I felt I just might have a choice in the direction I was headed. There was a true north, and I was going to chase it. Jesus was equipping me with a sail and rudder. It was time to learn these new tools so I could start using the wind and waves of this world to my advantage.

God was no longer this religious thing I viewed and judged from a distance. He was alongside—and even inside—me, coaxing and coaching me. In a way, He was teaching me how to navigate.

For someone who had always emphasized belonging to a tribe or being part of a group, I had an important lesson to learn. Not only could I never hope to earn God's love, but I also couldn't go through life dependent on other people's acceptance. This became clear to me when I went to a Promise Keepers rally.

Thousands of Christian men filled the venue in Grand Rapids, Michigan. There were lots of cheers for Jesus and enthusiastic singing, with guys waving their hands in the air like it was a cross between a rock concert and a football game. The speakers were all pumped, challenging the crowd to get right with God and live faithful lives as husbands and fathers. Men around me were in tears as they acknowledged different struggles, from alcohol and porn to being addicted to their work.

This was all a new experience for me and a long way from what I was used to at St. Martha Parish. I didn't want to get cynical, and while I couldn't fault what I was hearing, I just didn't feel comfortable with all the emotional high-fiving and so on.

God was working on me in a quieter way. I was learning about Him in times of stillness and reflection, not amid a lot of noise.

I came to understand that God doesn't always speak in a booming voice or with a blinding light. After reading about Him in the Old Testament, I found that I identified with the prophet Elijah. God told him to go and stand on a mountain, where he experienced a great wind, an earthquake, and a fire.

"But the LORD was not in [them]," the Bible says

(1 Kings 19:11–12). A gentle whisper followed, and that was when Elijah heard God. It was mostly the same for me.

I had started working out again. Instead of listening to music as I once did to pump me up, I'd exercise in silence. I began to tune in to what was going on inside, allowing space for ideas to rise and gel. This was not just abstract musings about faith and God but practical wrestling with what it meant to live in a way that reflected my growing beliefs.

One example of this was when I read in the Bible where Jesus told His disciples they should love their neighbor. That had always sounded noble and sweet until I realized Jesus meant this not as a vague concept but as a concrete action. It involved looking at how I actually felt about my next-door neighbor.

One neighbor came across as cold and condescending. I would do all I could to avoid her. *Why take the time to be nice to someone who angers and frustrates me?* I then read how Jesus wasn't impressed by people who were kind only to people they liked. Even pagans did that, Jesus pointed out.

It was a Saturday morning when the lesson finally sank in. I was on our roof, using a blower to clear the sticks and leaves that had collected over the winter. I glanced at my crabby neighbor's house and saw the same mess on her roof. A little voice inside said, *Go over and offer to do hers.*

I argued with myself for a few moments before I gave in. My neighbor looked surprised—and suspicious—when she answered the door.

"Hey," I said brightly. "I was blowing the sticks and leaves off my roof when I looked over and saw you've got a bunch on yours. I've got my ladder and blower out—would you like me to clear your roof for you?"

She thought for a moment. "Sure," she said. As she closed the door, she muttered, "Don't blow any of it on my car."

Her less-than-warm response took me aback for a moment. Then I realized that was part of the lesson. We don't treat people well because it makes us feel good or because they will say nice things about us. We treat people well because we are all children of God.

Jesus died for all of us—even the crabby ones.

We become the light of God to shine on all whether they are grateful or not. Matthew 5:45 says, "That you may be children of your Father in heaven. He causes his sun to rise on the evil and the good, and sends rain on the righteous and the unrighteous" (NIV).

Another way in which I found myself changing was in my use of words. I had always possessed a fairly sharp sense of humor and a quick wit, but I began to dial it back. It became apparent to me that, yes, sarcasm was a way of making people laugh but it was most often at the expense of someone else.

A whole new dimension to my life opened up after I took my step of faith in the weight room that day. It was as though the world began to morph from two dimensions to three, or from black and white to color. I realized there was so much more going on than I had previously known. My spiritual awareness was at an all-time high.

Take Aunt Helen. She was one of Grandma Sorber's younger sisters who lived in Binghamton, New York. Her husband had died when they were both still young, and she had never remarried. Aunt Helen would visit from time to time, and some of my earliest memories of her revolve around how much interest she showed in us kids. She would sit and listen to our stories, making me feel warm because of the attention she gave.

Sometime after I'd begun working on my faith journey, I was chatting with Grandma Sorber when she mentioned she'd been talking to Aunt Helen. "She just wanted me to be sure to tell you that she prays for you every day."

I was rocked. First, I didn't know she was still alive. Second, I had no idea that anyone in our family believed in God the way I had come to believe. I was surprised and touched.

I thought how neat it was to know that someone had been praying for me all those years when I was unaware of it and how they had probably been part of bringing me to where I was. It made me realize that our lives are such a tapestry, interwoven with events and other people. Some patterns and purposes are all too easy to miss when we are wrapped up in our own lives.

During that process, I also came to recognize how important Fran's faith had been in our journey. Though Fran had not been especially vocal about what she believed, I always knew that faith ran deep and true inside her. She had an unspoken conviction. Her quiet belief had shored us up so often and in so many ways. Now, taking a cue from me talking about what I was reading and thinking, Fran began to speak more freely about her faith. I was fascinated to hear about the certainty she had long enjoyed—a certainty I had taken for granted.

What I was learning outside the Catholic church through influential Protestant writers such as C. S. Lewis enriched and strengthened what I was experiencing at St. Martha Parish. I never felt a tension between the two. Understanding the Bible was making services at St. Martha much more meaningful. When I viewed its beautiful stained glass windows, I recognized the passages they celebrated—appreciating them not just as works of art but as statements of faith.

My life settled as I became more comfortable living with the changes I was making. I started questioning how I spent my time. What was I reading?

What was I watching on TV or at the movies?

And why did I spend time with certain people while avoiding others?

I also questioned the things that occupied my thoughts. I wasn't policing myself—I was protecting myself from what could cause me unnecessary harm. Some adjustments were easy, such as treating my family, friends, and even strangers better than I had before. I also found it painless to cut out certain shows and movies from my life.

Cutting ties with negative friends and observing how some of these people called less and less made me feel relieved. These developments affirmed that I was headed in the right direction. However, some things were more difficult, such as eliminating my salty language and sharp tongue. But I was making progress.

Yes, I was feeling good. I was going in a true north direction. All I could see were the positive changes in my life, which made me slightly blind to a small blip on the radar. The kind you get warned about on The Weather Channel. A small, low-pressure system spinning off in a remote part of the Atlantic Ocean.

CHAPTER NINE

No More Hiding

GOD WILL GUIDE me around any storm in my life, correct?

That was my assumption during this honeymoon phase of my newfound faith. I found out a little later that God equips us to be storm fighters, not storm avoiders. The winds began to snap the flags of my life when a neighbor introduced me to Mike Winter.

Mike played an important part setting the foundation for my newfound faith and launching me out to share that faith with others. Mike was leading a group called the Christian Business Men's Connection (CBMC). This organization is all over the United States and in one hundred countries, representing men who love God and want to serve Him well through their businesses. One of many things CBMC does is get together for lunches, where they invite other men in business along to hear Christian speakers.

One day Mike came by the Two Men and a Truck office, and I told him my story. He listened with interest and then asked if I'd like to get involved with CBMC's Operation Timothy, a program that helps new believers anchor their faith. Hungry for input and taking this as another resource God was giving me, I told him sure.

We met regularly to discuss questions I had, and Mike recommended several helpful books that became part of my growth. Then he threw out a challenge that really stretched me. Mike wanted me to tell my story at a CBMC luncheon in front of about a hundred people.

I instantly felt nauseous as memories of my time at Northern Michigan University came rushing back. That whole memory of the crash-and-burn presentation and the ensuing talk with Dr. Joyle filled my head like rushing water.

"Your story will help a lot of guys, Brig." Mike explained, his voice snapping me back into the present moment.

"I'm sorry, but no way," I said. "Just speaking to a dozen people or so at a Two Men and a Truck franchise scares the hell out of me."

Mike wouldn't take no for an answer. He asked me to pray about it. I reluctantly agreed to pray and was dismayed to sense God saying to me, *Do it, Brig.*

My apprehension only got worse when Mike told me I should plan on speaking for about thirty to forty-five minutes—that sounded like an eternity. I wrote my story down and practiced it many times. Mike pulled together a few guys for a trial-run presentation, which helped. They gave me some useful feedback and encouragement.

Still, as the event drew near, I was feeling more and more nervous. A few days before the luncheon, I got home from work and went up to our bedroom. I lay on the floor and burst into tears as all the pent-up anxiety came rushing out. I'd been learning that prayer wasn't just for meals or church services. It was an opportunity to talk to God anytime, anywhere. So I spoke up. I told God I was scared to death, that I couldn't stand public speaking, and that I didn't want to do this. It felt good to let everything out.

I paused, breathing heavily, my heart racing. Then I sensed God speaking to me. *Don't worry. Remember, you will do this through My strength, not yours. I'm with you. We are going to help a lot of people. Don't be afraid.*

This gave me the assurance I needed to regroup. I went back to my script and did some editing before rehearsing the presentation again. When the day of the luncheon finally arrived, I wasn't exactly calm and confident, but I was committed to seeing it through. My last prayer before I went out to speak was simple: *Please, God, don't let me turn green.*

Facing the hundred-plus people in the room, I made a joke about not being a public speaker as a way of explaining why I'd be referring to my notes. Then I started to read at a bit of a gallop. Mike, sitting in the front row, caught my eye. He was making frantic *slow down* signals at me.

I took a few deep breaths and found my rhythm. When I finally reached the halfway point, I thought that maybe I could get to the end without passing out. I realized that though I may not have been particularly polished, people seemed to be listening to what I had to say.

Encouraged, I wrapped up my story and closed with a prayer. It echoed the one I'd whispered on my weight bench. I invited anyone listening who wanted to come to know Jesus, as I had, to repeat it after me.

Later Mike came up to me very excited. They had collected response cards from the crowd, and twenty-five of them had indicated that they had repeated my prayer and wanted to know more about being a Christian. I couldn't believe it.

"Brig, your story connects with people," Mike said. "The fact that you're not a 'professional' public speaker is an asset. You're real, and people see that. These guys are in business, and they know a sales pitch when they hear one. That's not what you gave them. You spoke from the heart."

I was relieved that I had gotten through the presentation and it had borne fruit. But my momentary reprieve was quickly overshadowed when Mike talked about me doing it again. I sensed that God thought this was a good idea—which meant more speaking engagements.

Anyone who thinks that becoming a Christian is a cop-out to avoid dealing with the real world has never really studied the Bible. As I read it more and more, I realized the Bible wasn't a book of fluffy fables, as some people have argued. It deals with humanity at its worst—violent, immoral, selfish. Even the heroes are flawed. Yet through it all runs a message of hope that God still loves the world and hasn't given up on us.

I began to see Jesus in a different light. He wasn't this meek and mild guy wandering around with a sheep draped around His neck, telling everyone to be nice and get along. His love wasn't wishy-washy. It was fierce. He didn't mince His words, and He certainly wasn't afraid to get in people's faces.

I felt God placing me in front of a mirror. Through the example of Jesus's time on earth, God showed me my heart and where He would like to direct it. *Was I really living in a way that reflected His love and truth?* This question went deep into every part of my life— from what I believed about value and success, to how I treated those I loved, to the way that we ran the business. I knew that my actions had to match up with what I said. I had to walk the talk.

This lesson was driven home to me by a priest, but not in a positive way. I knew him from a Catholic church in the area, so when he called to ask for help with a local move, I set him up with our Lansing office.

After the job, I got a call from the office manager. The Two Men and a Truck crew had turned up at the priest's home and asked him if he could clean up some of the items they were moving. The items were dirty, and it's part of the protocol to ensure that everything is in good condition before it gets loaded.

The priest lost it, screaming and shouting with the most unholy terms at the movers. At one point, they even feared he was going to get physically violent with them. The Lansing manager, who I knew was a Christian, was shaken as he told me about the experience.

"Worst of all, Brig," he said, "one of the movers said that if that's what being a Christian is all about, then he didn't want anything to do with it."

I was really upset. Since I had become a true believer, I had tried to live my faith in all aspects of my life, not just at home. I didn't force the Bible down anyone's throat, but I wasn't apologetic either. I made it clear what I believed. So to have a man of the cloth, someone I respected, serve as such a poor example made me very sad.

After a lengthy prayer and with a shaky hand, I called the priest. When he recognized my voice, he said that he presumed I was calling to apologize for the difficulty with the crew.

"Actually, no," I told him. I had high regard for the priesthood, but I couldn't just let this go and say nothing.

"Honestly, I'm a little disappointed," I went on. "They came back and told me that you had treated them very poorly, Father. I respect you and love you, but I've been working hard to bring people to Christ at work. I now have a mover—maybe two—who said that if this is what it means to be a Christian, they don't want anything to do with it."

There was a moment's silence.

"Thank you for saying that, Brig. I appreciate it," he said quietly. We both had a newfound respect for each other from that moment on.

Though I knew I had to call him out on that, I did so with fear and trembling. I understood I was—and remain to this day—a work in progress. There were many ways in which I felt God prodding me to clean up my own act. Fortunately, life seems to give us plenty of chances to get things right.

Driving home from the office one fall evening, my car was hit by a beautiful six-point buck that sprang from the woods. He caught our Chevy Astro on the driver's side door, rocking the vehicle and shocking the life out of me. I took the van to a friend's auto body shop. He looked at the damage and wrote up a quote for the insurance company that included repairing the side along with some dings on the front and rear. I told him the dings on the front and rear were already there.

"Yeah, that's okay," he said. "The insurance will cover it."

When I told him that wouldn't work for me, we got into a bit of a debate. He said that it was no big deal— the insurance firm had that sort of thing figured into their algorithm. They knew people did it all the time.

"Maybe," I said, "But that's not my algorithm. I'll pay for the other repairs myself."

I did not make these decisions just to be a good boy. It sends a direct message to God when we cheat on our taxes or insurance claims. When we take advantage of a stranger or even a family member, it says to God, "Your grace and blessings are not enough for me."

Some of the ways in which I sensed God refining me took longer to learn. As much as I loved my children, I often felt that Fran was too easygoing with them or that she let things pass when she should have been firmer. I thought she sometimes rushed in to help them too quickly, when they really needed to learn about consequences. It was a quiet bone of contention between us for some time.

I didn't realize that my reaction to her patience and tenderness revealed more about me than it did about Fran. When I began to understand how much God loved me, it led to a revelation. One day when I mumbled something about Fran spoiling the kids, she told me, "I'm not spoiling them, Brig. I'm loving them."

The lights finally went on. I realized Fran was right. It occurred to me that what may have been my norm was maybe not the right norm. In the light of this "aha" moment, I made a conscious effort to get more involved with my kids. In my new relationship with God, I found He was a loving father, not a cop. Maybe I should follow suit.

This change of perspective regarding Fran and the kids was part of a broader shift going on inside me. As I became more and more secure in knowing God loves me for who I am—not for anything I had ever done or could ever hope to do for Him—I realized I didn't have to run for cover when bad things came up. I didn't have to hide from Him or anyone else.

In fact, over time, I came to welcome some of the challenges and difficulties. I recognized that they were opportunities to learn more about God. This would prove to be an important lesson for what was ahead in my role at Two Men and a Truck.

CHAPTER TEN

Faith Under Fire

ONE OF THE GREAT THINGS about the professional moving industry is that the physical component is challenging to automate. Moving belongings in and out while being aware of each person's unique desires makes every moving experience unique. This results in a business model that relies on people.

Stick Men University˚, our training department named after the two stick men in our logo, was located at our Two Men and a Truck headquarters. Just as fire departments have faux homes for running drills and the military has fake city settings in which to train, we had a "house" where new franchises could bring their leaders to train them how to become professional movers.

There were steps up to the front door of number 1985—a nod to the year Two Men and a Truck was formally established by my mom while I was off at college. Inside, a fully outfitted laundry room, kitchen, living room, bedroom, and office were all packed into the moving house from hell. The furniture included puffy leather sofas, chairs, cabinets, a fireproof safe, and a grand piano. Everything had to be maneuvered down a curving, tight staircase with a low-hanging chandelier and loaded carefully into the truck box mounted at the appropriate height outside.

To keep students on their toes, each move would offer problem-solving challenges. There would be fake prescription drugs left on a bedroom dresser, a toy handgun tucked between a mattress, and a plastic bag of oregano—imitating a bag of pot—under the piano cover. They had to use their training to know the best way to handle each discovery.

On one occasion, I joked with the person supervising the training class about all the scuff marks on the walls and ceiling where the new movers had been careless with items. "What's up with all of that?" I asked. "We just had this all patched and painted."

"Better here than in someone's home," he replied.

While Two Men and a Truck offered training well beyond anything Jon and I received on those first moves we did as kids, there was no faux house for leadership training.

As the person responsible for bringing in new franchisees, I had grown close with many of them. I understood the jump they had made. They had their own "burn the boats" moment, and I felt like I was the one who handed them the matches.

Two Men and a Truck had built a winning system, but that didn't mean the franchisee's experience would be easy. It was not uncommon for a new franchisee to quit their job, sell their house, pull their kids from school, and move to another state in a matter of months.

Before moving forward with a new franchisee, we made sure we were confident they were making the right decision. Two Men and a Truck would be there for them, holding their hands until they were walking, then running. As we added more franchises over the years, I was fortunate to warm my hands over all those boat-burning fires.

As the franchisees became established, they added more services, employees, and equipment. This was a learning experience we all went through together. Our corporate office—along with our franchisees—determined that Two Men and a Truck would be "the company that never made it." *Whenever you think you have made it, you are done.* If we were not growing, we were dying. We became comfortable being uncomfortable.

Like many leaders, I continued to hone my skills and grow both personally and professionally. Careers are all about adding more responsibility and taking ownership of opportunities that come along. My opportunity came in the spring of 2008 when I was asked to take over the company's day-to-day leadership. I was offered the position of company president and would eventually take on the role of CEO. This was something I wanted, but I knew I could not do it alone. The first thing I did after accepting the job offer was to ask God for help.

I remembered reading in 2 Chronicles 1:10 when King David's son Solomon had come to the throne, he had asked first for wisdom—not riches or fame—which pleased God. So I echoed Solomon's prayer. Then I read and reread Proverbs, the Old Testament book of wise sayings that was mostly written and compiled by King Solomon.

There are thirty-one chapters in the book of Proverbs. A good friend told me his dad suggested he read a Proverbs chapter every night. I took his advice and learned words to live by—my favorite being Proverbs 12:24: "Work hard and become a leader; be lazy and become a slave" (NLT). This verse was written over three thousand years ago but sounds like it was penned last week. I was amazed at how timeless the insights were and how often I could apply them to my own leadership challenges.

I was both nervous and excited about taking the helm. We had some big challenges ahead, but I had confidence that God had been grooming me for this opportunity. I knew the business well, and I was putting down firm roots in my faith.

Any gardener will tell you that it requires good, well-balanced soil for a seed to take root. Two Men and a Truck's roots were strong. We successfully provided a service our customers needed, we instilled time-tested values, and we had a solid group of franchisees as our partners.

But there was a problem. We needed a larger planter box. The seeds that had been cultivated and watered were outgrowing the size of the pot, and we didn't have the resources to expand. When multiple cracks in our support system appeared, we didn't just end up with a cracked pot—it was broken. I was spending more and more time putting out fires, assuring complaining franchisees that we were working on the various issues. I tried my best to remind them of all the positive ways we were helping them, but the discontent was rising.

There were many challenges, but I knew the first thing we needed to address was our IT department. For a multilocation franchise operation, this was our central nervous system. When Fran and I ran our small franchise in northern Michigan, we were able to schedule all our jobs on paper or maybe on a whiteboard. But we had grown beyond the ability to manage jobs that way, especially for our multilocation franchises. Our IT system was crucial to their success.

This IT system—called the Movers Who Care system—was built in the late '90s. Movers Who Care allowed our franchisees to grow tremendously, but we couldn't hope to function to the best of our abilities if it were compromised.

Our marketing director at the time suggested we ask Plante Moran, an accounting and business advisory group, to come in and evaluate things. The review didn't come cheap, but it was some of the best money we've ever spent. I asked the point man for the project, Jon Nobis, to explain things in plain

English for me—my urban planning degree wouldn't help me much, but I did know the value of open and honest feedback and that sometimes you have to seek a different perspective.

Nobis suggested assigning grades like the ones in school. I agreed. At the end of this six-week review, he started with hardware: F. We weren't even using standardized computers in the home office, let alone in the franchise locations.

"Your hardware is outdated," he said. "You have no industry standards. You don't even have a firewall. I'm surprised no one's brought the whole thing down yet."

It got worse.

Software: F. "Did you know that some of the programs you're using are pirated?" He told me we had sixty thousand dollars in new software sitting unopened on the computer room floor—it had been there for months.

Many of our IT personnel were to be commended for the way they had managed to keep the whole system running. But they were so busy resolving everyday problems that they didn't have time to work on long-term solutions. The proposed fix involved cutting-edge ideas that would require a significant investment. And even the big capital expenditure was more like a shot at success than it was a guarantee.

Finally, Jon came to the contractors who had created the Movers Who Care system for us.

Another F.

"They don't have a source code for it," Nobis told me.

He explained that our system was developed using outdated software as the foundation. It also lacked documentation. When things went wrong, they couldn't go in and fix them. We were using workaround solutions, and that's why the system kept crashing.

I was stunned and energized at the same time. The assessment was damning, but at least I knew the scale of the problem, what needed to change, and what kind of urgency we were dealing with.

The Plante Moran report highlighted a broader issue we faced: making the transition from a scrappy start-up to a big business. The style that had been our strength in the early days could not sustain us into the future. Our system and processes had performed well for us as a smaller institution, but they would not work as we continued to grow.

Changes needed to be made to keep up with the times and scale of our operations. Either we were going to pay now or pay the price at harvest time. Our seeds of success were being choked off by an inability to invest in technology and people.

Meanwhile, we had to be ready to pump money into solving the IT crisis—that meant new hires and new equipment. I wasn't too worried because I knew we had the resources. Sometime back, on our banker's advice, we had transferred three million dollars sitting in our checking account and put it into a money market fund to earn interest.

The banker called and wanted to take me to lunch. He mainly chit-chatted about golf. I told him we would need to tap into the money market fund to upgrade our corporate office computers. He said he would reach out to me in a week.

When he called, he said there was a problem. It turned out we didn't have those funds in a money market fund—they were in a type of bond known as auction rate securities (ARS). These were long-term bonds intended to behave somewhat like a money market fund. Even though the bonds were technically long term, the securities were supposed to be highly liquid, with a certain amount being sold each week during investor auctions. The interest rate that investors received was reset through these ongoing investor auctions.

As the financial crisis deepened, the auction market for those types of securities collapsed. There were no buyers, which meant we couldn't cash out our investment. That also meant the issuer of the bonds had no way to determine what interest payments to make. We might never see that money again, our banker explained apologetically.

I found out later that the week before when we were having lunch, other bankers were frantically trying to get their clients out of these funds. I was stunned.

"Do you realize that this is the working capital for our business?" I snapped. Without getting our hands on those funds, we had maybe six months' worth of cash left at best. Another unexpected challenge had hit me.

"I don't know what to say," he answered. "This is the first time this has ever happened."

I sat at my desk in a state of disbelief, staring aimlessly for a few moments before eventually being overtaken with laughter. I had prided myself on trusting God since taking over as president. As a sign of my relinquishing control, I had begun to start each day by saying, "Okay, God, what do You want me to do with *Your* moving business today?" I prayed about every decision, and I sensed His lead and direction as I made tough calls.

As the news of our mishandled nest egg sank in, I realized I had not been trusting God fully—I had been leaning on this cash crutch sitting in what I thought was a money market account. Now that crutch had been kicked out from under me.

I was not laughing like a madman on the brink of a breakdown—rather more at my foolish, half-hearted faith. Yes, I was asking the Lord, "What are we going to do in Your moving business today?" But deep down, I knew that we had a vast pot of dry powder sitting at the bank, waiting to be tapped. Scripture states, "You know my sitting down and my rising up; You understand my thought afar off" (Psalm 139:2).

My faith was still strong enough to know that God had another, better plan. Jeremiah 29:11 says, "'For I know the plans I have for you,' declares the LORD, 'plans to prosper you and not to harm you, plans to give you hope and a future'" (NIV).

With this promise, I prayed again, "*Now*, what do You want to do in Your moving business today?" Psalm 46:10 came to mind: *Be still, and know that I am God.*

I thought about the panicked line we have all heard: "Don't just stand there, do something!" That particular day I flipped the saying to "Just stand there and do nothing—God's got this!" With that, I placed my computer in my backpack, shut the lights off, and went home for the day. It was going to be okay.

CHAPTER ELEVEN

Removing the Stumps

DESPITE THE INTERNAL challenges we were facing, the business continued to grow. We were adding franchises at an unprecedented rate. Existing franchises were buying additional trucks and hiring more staff. We had recently built a new, multimillion-dollar corporate office complete with a quarter-million-dollar windmill for backup power. In the lobby of our modern new building, we proudly displayed back-to-back J.D. Power and Associates trophies for customer satisfaction awards we had won in the mid-2000s.

They wouldn't remain there much longer.

The painful recession of 2008 finally exposed our broken systems. As things got tight for many people financially, they were no longer just calling in and picking a date and a time to move. They were price shopping. This was new to many of our franchises' customer service representatives (CSRs) who scheduled the moving jobs.

During the housing boom of the early 2000s, the CSRs had gradually defaulted to acting as order takers. Now many of them could not sell our value. This turned out to be a huge problem as customers increasingly looked for the cheapest price.

At the same time, more customers began using the internet to communicate with us.

Unfortunately, we were getting relatively few lead conversions from the increased online activity. We could not figure out why that was the case so we hired an outside company to help. They captured the email addresses of people who visited our site. Then they sent a questionnaire asking the prospective client why they did not use our services. The feedback:

"You suck!"

"You never got back to me."

"Your site is too hard to navigate."

"It froze up every time I tried to use it."

And on and on. We later discovered the site had over an eighty percent drop-off rate. Many customers gave up or were timed off from the site—we were losing literally thousands of leads every week.

Our overall volume of inquiries began going down as the recession deepened, exposing our brokenness even more. All this was happening while our franchisee management software was in its final death throes— unsupported by code and hosted on individual franchisee servers, many of which were beyond their intended life. Our franchisees were losing patience.

The smell of business death hung in the air like hot roadkill on the highway. If there was any encouragement to be found, it was that not all the stench was coming from us. Several other moving companies in our markets were shutting down and other industries were experiencing a similar storm.

Only customer-centric businesses that could aggressively adjust were surviving.

With all the doom-and-gloom economic commentary and forecasts on the news every day, I knew that we needed to offer some sort of hope—something for everyone to rally around. It came from an unlikely source: my dad. Though he never had any involvement with the company, he unintentionally gave me what I was needing.

A group of us, including my dad, were having a spring "working bee" at our remote hunting camp in the Upper Peninsula of Michigan. The rustic log cabin, with its outdoor, woodburning sauna, overlooked a large beaver-dammed lake. In the fall, we would row across the lake to the best deer hunting spot on the property.

We were shocked when we rolled up to the camp that night. The body of water that was once a lake had been reduced to nothing but a small, meandering creek. It was a wasteland of logs, stumps, and branches. Below-average winter snows—which led to very little snow melt and a broken beaver dam—were the main culprits. It was disturbing to see what our boat had been floating over during periods of higher water.

As we leaned against our four-wheelers nursing beers, Dad looked over at the partially submerged obstacle course and said, "This would be the time to pull all that shit out of there. With the water this low, we can see all the hang-ups." I immediately thought of the business.

"What did you say?" I asked.

"We should get a strap and a four-wheeler down there and pull that crap out," he said. "Anything that can't be dragged, we cut out with a chain saw. Look at it! It's all exposed. Hell, if we only get half the water back, we can still make it across the pond."

"Oh, man. Dad, that's brilliant!" I said out loud as my thoughts went back to Two Men and a Truck.

"Not *that* brilliant, Brig," he protested as he walked off, thinking I was making fun of him.

I sat and finished my beer, thinking of all the parallels of the pond and Two Men and a Truck. The stumps, logs, and branches were metaphors of our broken processes. The water depth symbolized the volume of business. The leaking beaver dam? Waste.

The next day, we did what Dad suggested. With chainsaws, straps, four-wheelers, and an Argo ATV, we attacked everything that would stop a boat from going across a partially filled pond. We would be ready the following year when average precipitation put water back in the pond and the beavers did their repair work.

We didn't clear it all out, but we removed enough to cut a large swath that would allow us to navigate a rowboat to the other side.

Fast forward three months to March 2009. When I stepped up to the whiteboard at our annual meeting event in Sacramento, California, I still had an image of all of the debris banging the bottom of our boat in a shallow pond fresh in my mind. These events were usually a blast with the combined feel of anticipation of spring weather and a family reunion.

We would introduce new procedures and practices while celebrating successes and socializing. But this year was much more somber. We were worried. Was this a blip on the financial radar or the start of something cataclysmic?

Taking a marker, I began drawing on the whiteboard. First, I sketched a cross-section of a pond with lots of logs and branches down at the bottom. Then I drew a high-water line so that the debris was well below the surface. I added a boat gliding over the logs and other debris. Next, I erased the existing line for the water level and drew it lower, so the submerged stuff started to hit the hull of the boat.

"The problem isn't the water level," I said. "That's out of our hands. It may never again rise as high as it used to be, for all we know. The answer is not to focus on how much the water has dropped but on what's under the surface. If we can clear out whatever is in the way below the surface, we can get to the other side again. We can still navigate the boat in less water."

"That's what we are going to do right now. We

need to pull the stumps out of our way—things like getting our technology upgraded, building a functioning website, better sales processes and training, new skill sets, stronger budgeting and planning, and all of our teams working together more efficiently. We can be profitable with fewer moves. We can get more of the 'less' moving that is still going on out there—if we work smarter and eliminate some of the obstacles."

The visual image seemed to connect with people. I could sense the atmosphere had lightened a little at our evening mixer. We weren't out of the woods, but we'd given them hope that there was a route we could follow. It would require effort, but we weren't helpless victims. We didn't have to wait for someone else to rescue us. We could take active steps of our own.

It was time to clear the stumps. The recession was not our problem—the recession had simply exposed our problems. A few days after our return from Sacramento, I woke up, looked in the mirror, smiled, and said out loud, "You suck!"

It didn't hurt—it was a relief. I went into the office, grabbed the J.D. Power and Associates trophies that were prominently displayed on the front desk, and handed them to Norma, our receptionist. I told her to put them away in the closet with the Christmas decorations.

"Why?" she asked.

"Because we suck!" I told her.

She shrugged, grabbed the hardware, and made her way to the closet. It was liberating. No longer would we look out the window at the storm, wringing our hands, glaring at all the things beyond our control. Now we were looking into the mirror at the things we could do something about.

There is something energizing about knowing you have some control over a situation, even if it means just taking small steps. I was reminded of our house back in Ishpeming. Rather than worrying about what we couldn't control, we decided to focus on what we could.

Okay, so there was less moving going on in the world. We couldn't change that. But we could improve the way we did things so that we got to do more of the "less" moving going on. If we closed a decent percentage of those fizzled online leads, we would still be growing. I pulled our home office executives into a meeting and told them we sucked.

"Our short-term goal is not to be great," I announced. "It's to suck less."

Part of Two Men and a Truck's success and appeal had been in giving people opportunities to make something of themselves—from those starting franchises to the home office staff. Leaders at our company headquarters had all started in entry-level positions and worked their way up. But some now carried responsibilities that had outgrown their abilities. I knew we

155

needed to bring in people from the outside to take over a few key leadership areas.

The woman I hired to take over the IT department was a no-nonsense, hard-charging type who knew her stuff—just the kind of person to help us rescue the areas of our business that were in danger.

She brought in some needed processes and industry standards. We revamped our websites and put franchise training together on how to manage internet leads. We used the equivalent of duct tape and baling wire to stabilize our Movers Who Care management software. At the same time, we worked on building our new, single-platform Movers Who Care 2 system. We were patching a sinking boat in a stormy ocean while building a new ship next to it.

Next we profiled our top CSRs, looking for standard, positive traits. Franchisees used these profiles to put the right people on the phones and computers for internet leads. From there, we hired a company to comb through all the processes involved in working with a customer. We documented every step—from taking the first call to when the truck pulled away after completing a successful move. When we finished, we had a scroll of paper measuring over twelve feet long.

Then we began looking for bottlenecks in our processes.

Within months, we began to suck less. Meanwhile, we started to get calls from savvy investors looking to buy panicking businesses for pennies on the dollar. I could picture grumpy old Mr. Potter from *It's a Wonderful Life* on the phone sitting behind a big oak desk in a stuffy office. My slightly dark humor helped me get through. The would-be buyers usually asked if I had received their letter inquiring about purchasing our business.

"Why would you want to buy us?" I would answer. "We suck. We're not worth anything."

There would be silence on the other end of the line.

Part of sucking less involved narrowing our focus and concentrating on areas where we traditionally excelled. This required reassessing our expansion plans. In an attempt to enter key markets where we had zero or little brand presence—such as California, Texas, and Washington—we targeted our corporately owned Two Men and a Truck locations.

The original strategy had seemed sound at the time. We knew those markets had tremendous potential, so rather than trying to find someone to assume the risk of opening a franchise, we decided to begin with family-owned locations in pivotal cities. The idea was that we could establish a foundation on which we could build.

Those locations never took off.

We didn't know the markets well enough to be successful. We lacked boots-on-the-ground ownership working in the specific operations each day. Sure, we had financial control several hundred miles away, but there is a different perspective when an owner is unlocking the doors to the office each morning.

We also didn't have the proper resources from a corporate standpoint to help manage the locations. We hemorrhaged money for several years before finally pulling the plug—either through transferring those locations to actual franchise owners or shutting them down completely. The franchisees who took on those markets built up the brand and continue to do so today.

Even more ambitiously, we had been looking beyond the United States. *Other franchises had gone global so why not Two Men and a Truck?* Well, because not all industries are easily translatable, as it turned out.

We had initially been excited at the prospect, even developing an international logo with the original two stick men and their truck overlaid on a globe that Mom made. I had accompanied Mom on a trip to Asia in 2003 when the International Franchise Association (IFA) asked her to be part of a group to talk about business opportunities for women. It soon became apparent, however, that there is more to exporting a business than merely translating our words.

Through our meetings and discussions, it was evident that getting Two Men and a Truck going in Asia would be hard for several reasons (at least in the early 2000s). Those reasons ranged from government regulations and traffic issues to the simple fact that, in many places, people just didn't own as much stuff as we do in the Western world. We met with several seriously interested parties in China, Singapore, and Thailand but decided not to pursue those markets.

We didn't abandon overseas expansion without further efforts, however. More westernized parts of the world seemed to offer greater opportunities. We sent one of our top young trainers, Randy Shacka—who would eventually become the Two Men and a Truck president—to South Africa to help establish an operation there.

From everything we could gather, the country was well positioned for us. But we ran into all kinds of problems. Technology kept failing. There was difficulty finding suitable trucks and key vendor relationships. Government restrictions prevented us from getting our royalty payments out of the country. After a year or so of headaches, we had to cut our losses.

Though we seriously pulled back on our international plans, we didn't give up entirely. We took the lessons we had learned and applied them to our most significant, albeit small-to-date, successes. In Canada we now have more than twenty-five locations operating under a master franchise model. We also have a franchise in Ireland and the United Kingdom, each directly supported by our home office in Michigan. They are more of a toehold than a foothold right now, but we anticipate slow and steady growth.

We continue to face the challenge of building brand awareness where Two Men and a Truck is a newcomer, especially where people commonly refer to trucks as "vans" and "lorries." Still, we have made much progress in proving that a viable model exists overseas.

Another area where we had overreached stood out to me every morning as I drove into the parking lot. It was that windmill on the edge of the property, towering a hundred and twenty feet in the air. More often than I'd care to remember, the giant blades were still, and we would have to call a repairman.

The windmill had been installed to great fanfare as a power source we could rely on when storms hit our local power grid. We were told that it wouldn't provide enough juice for the whole building but would keep our computer system running. That was important for our business needs and was a major selling point. We were even told that any power it generated that we didn't use could be bought back by the local power company.

Our green consciousness earned us some favorable publicity, at least at the local level. We even allowed schools to bring busloads of kids out to look. But when it came to functionality, the windmill was a bust. Many days it simply didn't work. When we asked the power company about selling them our excess wind-generated power, they said that while they wanted to do that kind of thing, they hadn't figured out how just yet.

I had voiced skepticism about the whole idea when it first came up but ultimately went along with the consensus view of our leadership team. By this point, however, with all the other issues we were dealing with, the windmill's presence bugged me. It felt like a giant middle finger raised at me every time I pulled into the parking lot.

Word got around that our eco-adventure hadn't gone well. Local business leaders, and even some of the people at our franchises, would jokingly ask me about our windmill. I quietly fumed. I'd had enough. If it had been made of wood, I might have burned the damn thing down myself. I asked the person in charge of our facilities to get it taken down or sell it on eBay—just get rid of it. After it was removed, we even broke up the giant concrete slab we had poured for the foundation. There would be no lingering evidence of this misstep.

I was reminded of an important lesson from all these challenges: You never make it. *Ever.* Customers' needs and wants are constantly changing. A shift or development in an industry that has nothing to do with ours can indirectly present us with a challenge. New technology opens all kinds of variants that can be embraced or ignored—but if you don't make a choice, one will be made for you. I found this holds true in our personal lives as well. We need a true north to base tough decisions on because they never stop coming.

Just like in business, we cannot simply ignore the hard choices and hope they go away. Doing nothing involves making a choice, and the results usually aren't pretty.

Overlooked decisions can end up becoming horrible solutions that take root in our lives.

Better to meet them head-on than leave them to chance. I would find this out soon enough, as I had a huge decision ahead of me.

CHAPTER TWELVE

In Deep Water

As I WALKED DOWN the narrow hall to the large meeting room at our corporate office, I sensed that familiar dread of having to speak in public—the one that had me turning green and feeling as if I were going to pass out. I was cold and sweaty at the same time.

When I opened the door, I instantly felt body heat slamming me in the face. Nervous people who had just witnessed someone else's nightmare stared back at me. I had released a third of our corporate office staff. Those who remained were thinking that it could have been their nightmare—and that it might still be. People were crying and shaking. There were angry stares but also looks of resolve. Everyone was waiting to hear what the hell just happened.

The short answer? We were in trouble.

I had known there were obstacles when I took over as president a year earlier. I just didn't know how deep these issues ran or how the recession would magnify them. After years of continuous growth, Two Men and a Truck had become the darling of the Lansing community and the IFA—but now we were reaching a crossroads.

Having started with our IT department, the

wobbles spread to operations. Frustrated franchisees, angry customers, and burned-out corporate employees sounded the alarm like a tornado warning before an oncoming storm. Our Movers Who Care IT system was continuously crashing, sending our franchisees into a panic. We could not fix these problems no matter how hard we tried.

Franchisees began to question the corporate office's competency—we were not bringing the value they needed to grow their businesses.

During this unsettling time, young talent departed our corporate office. One was a young man who was leaving Lansing for Chicago. I read his exit interview—he said he loved the company but he wasn't clear on everyone's role.

"For the life of me, three people in my department are a mystery," he said. "I have no clue what they do."

I took his comments seriously. There was no one to blame. It was a classic case of a small business getting very large in a hurry—we were falling over one another. I was proud of how far we had come as a company but as the business continued to scale, we needed industry standards in all departments and specific skill sets to establish and run those standards.

The business had been built by a savvy, hard-working corporate staff and by franchisees who ran with new ideas. In many ways, we were a different breed than what we are now. The people who comprised our system—both corporate and franchisee—were bruised and battle-tested. Working as we did was the only way we could have grown and stayed privately held. It was challenging, confrontational, and exhausting, but nobody was quitting, and we were growing every year.

I knew we needed to go deeper—there was more we could do to suck less. I remembered a colleague's advice from my days selling insurance. Bob Saari, an old Yooper, would yell, "Do something. Even if it's wrong!"

His point was that at least you'd be moving. I chose to move forward. On a large sheet of paper, I did my best to create an organizational chart matching each job description to an employee's name.

Then I took three highlighter markers and graded each position and person according to a stop-light rating system: green was good, yellow was not sure, red was no-go.

There were six leaders at the home office I knew were keepers. I brought them in and gave them each three colored markers and a copy of the organizational chart. I told them to do the same exercise I had done, but not to share their results yet. They had four days to work on it before we tallied everything into one combined chart.

To my amazement, the combined highlighted charts matched almost perfectly. We found a few very good employees whom we felt were in the wrong positions so we moved them to other roles. But it was evident we had some people we had to move out.

We didn't have a human resources department—another sign of how our growth had outstripped our capacity to manage well—so we called our outside payroll company for help. They suggested we rip the Band-Aid off and release all twenty-six people we had earmarked to go—all at the same time. This was not as difficult for me as I initially expected. So much so that I questioned my Christian faith. *Lord, am I a heartless leader? Is it all about the money?*

The decision became personal and emotional as I focused on individual people. In some cases, it brought tears to my eyes. I traced my steps back to how I had come to this conclusion.

First, there was prayer, and then counsel with Jon Nobis and Plante Moran. More prayer followed, along with the highlighting exercise and additional input from the home office leaders. In the end, I was confident this decision had been thoroughly prayed over and well-vetted.

In the meeting room with those who remained, I sat quietly for a moment and scanned the room. My thoughts went to a scribbled quote by John A. Shedd that lay under the clear plastic mat on my desk: "Ships are safe in port, but that is not what ships were built for."

This quote was something I had picked up at the IFA annual meeting many years ago. A sweaty, chubby little bald guy shared John A. Shedd's saying on an overhead projector as he riffled through a stack of transparent sheets. I remembered feeling glad that I wasn't him having to give a presentation, then being hit between the eyes with that quote. *Love that!* I grabbed a pen and wrote it down on the outline he had passed out.

I returned to this quote as I spoke to those in our corporate office who had managed to keep their jobs. "Ships are safe in port, but that's not what ships were built for," I said. "We are on the verge of business death. Our franchisees and our customers have just about had it. We are unable to sell our services in this tightening market, and our computers and software are old and obsolete. We are going to die in this place. Our Two Men and a Truck boat has been in port too long. We need to shove off, then cut barrels and roll them off the boat.

"Everything that is not essential needs to go, and we need to get out into the deep blue water. Our extravagant Christmas parties? Gone. Company picnics? Gone. The big buses to the Detroit Tigers baseball games? Gone. The six-week sabbatical program for employees who have been here for five years? Gone.

"We are not going to wait for the economic storm to blow over. Strap in people—we are going out into the storm. We *might* die out at sea, but we will *sure as hell* die sitting here.

"You need to know about the people who were let go," I continued. "That was hard for me. I cried several times over it, honestly. I bet I knew them better and longer than you did. They are not bad people; they are not incompetent. The job simply outgrew most of them—hell, it outgrew me. I will do everything in my power to help them find work. They have all been paid a severance.

"Look around you. Some of you will not be here this time next year. Not because you are going to be fired but because you will not be able to handle the work conditions it's going to require to save this company. When you chose to work for a moving franchise, you didn't think you were going to sign up for some crazy adventure, right? Well, guess what—you are in the middle of one now!"

I didn't speak very long, but I found myself standing by the time I finished, and my throat was hoarse from talking with so much emotion. The next day I pulled into the parking lot to find several empty spaces. I figured that would not be the only change I would notice.

Because it was a Wednesday, at noon I walked into the boardroom with a cup of coffee for the weekly Bible study. There was one other person there, a young lady from marketing. After five minutes went by, I asked where everyone was.

"You fired them all," she said.

"What?" I answered. "I wiped out our whole Bible study?" She just nodded.

I went back into my office, shut the door, shook my head, and laughed. I wasn't laughing over those who had been let go but in relief that God had kept me blind to the Bible study when we were making such tough decisions. I'd made the cuts purely on business grounds, not clouded by personal bias.

Some of those decisions were really hard. Several employees had been with us for years, from back when Two Men and a Truck was just a single location. They were part of our fabric. I had struggled to pull the trigger, knowing what I needed to do but not wanting to do it.

Then one morning after praying about these employees, God gave me peace about the decision. *Brig, it's OK to release them. I have other things they need to do. They are taking shelter here. Let them go.* This calmed my nerves and allowed me to move forward.

Still, not everyone was happy with what I was doing—a talented young lady from accounting quit. I was shocked and asked her not to leave, to give it some time. She said that what I had done was cruel. It dawned on me that not everyone would have handled the situation like I did.

At that time, I had an open-door policy that employees utilized. In the beginning, people were upset with the hard stance I took in letting people go. These were emotional conversations. Several employees were in tears. I appreciated their vulnerability and was glad that they felt free to be honest with me. I love frank conversations, and I learned to have a box of Kleenex handy on my desk.

A few of the staff were bold enough to say that I was destroying Two Men and a Truck's much-loved culture. I listened to what they had to say but disagreed with their conclusions. I said our culture was strangling us. Without the company there would be no culture. Our plan was to get healthy again—to make the company profitable for all who were willing to pound it out and risk it. And then I'd end our conversation with a question.

"Do you want to keep going to Tigers' games and picnics, or do you want to help reshape a company that will allow our system to grow stronger by supporting our franchisees to hire more people and put more trucks in more driveways?" I would then add, "By doing so, we are helping more customers. This, in turn, allows you to put meaningful dollars away for retirement, send your kids to college, and maybe buy a cottage on a lake someday."

The majority of people rallied. Over the next several months, the energy was high at the corporate office. There was an excitement I had never felt before. People began to thrive in the challenging atmosphere. They started taking ownership of their areas and making contributions to other departments. There was a sense of everyone being in this together.

I decided to host a pizza lunch for the whole corporate staff every six weeks. We would discuss our progress, and each department leader would report on what was happening in their area. These were very open conversations. We talked about challenges and wins.

After one of the meetings, I came up with the idea for an award. It would go to someone who went above and beyond, helping push our Two Men and a Truck boat out into the deep blue water.

Just thinking of that image stirred some of my earliest memories, such as fishing with Grandpa Sorber on Lake Charlevoix in northern Michigan. He had a twelve-foot aluminum boat with a 9-horse tiller motor. We fished for bluegill and perch.

Grandpa Sorber was originally from Chicago. He never wore jeans. He always dressed up, even for fishing. He wore brown slacks with a matching button-down shirt, dress shoes, and a brown dress hat. You honestly could not tell if he was going fishing or was about to sell an insurance policy.

As Grandpa Sorber steered the boat from the dock, I would sit at the bow and look down into the shallows. I loved the sound of that old aluminum boat cutting through the water. I could see everything on the bottom, from driftwood to rocks, from crayfish to darting minnows. As we ventured farther out, the water turned from light green to a deep blue, and I could no longer make out the shapes below.

How deep are we? I wondered. *What lies down there underneath the surface?* Putting a worm on the hook, I was hesitant to drop my line into the unknown.

Those mixed feelings from fishing with Grandpa Sorber long ago—excitement and adventure mixed with a splash of fear—come back into play when I think of the deep blue water. It was the perfect symbol for our company's new award.

To win a Deep Blue Water Award, an employee had to be nominated by someone from a department other than their own. Although the award was only a cheap gold plastic cup, it soon became prized. As the months went by, these accolades began to accumulate on desks around the office. One young lady soon had five of them prominently displayed on her desk. Wherever I spotted a collection of this plastic hardware, I knew we had found an ass-kicker and a winning team member.

Over time, we began to reintroduce some of the things we had nixed, but at a level more fitting of our situation. The company picnic was held in the parking lot with a couple of cases of beer and a corn hole tournament. People brought dishes to share. It was low budget but we had a blast.

Instead of a formal dinner at a high-end restaurant, we held our Christmas party in the office. We stopped work at 11:00 a.m. Once again, everyone had a dish to pass around. A guy from IT brought in some of his best homebrew.

We also held a euchre tournament and played Christmas shows on the big screens around the building. The next day, several employees came into my office and said it was the best Christmas party ever. They wanted to have the party at the office from now on. Other than having it catered, the Christmas party still looks and feels the same today as it did when we made the change.

There were other surprising upside developments that came out of our troubles. By the time we finished saying goodbye to people, we had only a few months' worth of cash left in the bank. It was a risk, but one I believed God would honor.

As it turned out, trimming our sails and offloading unnecessary cargo made our financial state much healthier. As more time went by, it was increasingly evident that taking Two Men and a Truck out of port and into deep blue water had safeguarded the company.

By reducing our workforce, we saved a considerable amount of money on salaries. This also prompted us to review and restructure ongoing wages. We brought in a human resources manager to help ensure our personnel processes were sound. She, along with the IT department head and our new CFO, helped us find more areas to save money.

As we reread the small print of some of the contracts we had with our suppliers, we discovered we were being taken advantage of in a big way. One seemingly minor example: We were being charged four dollars a page for printed reports from one vendor. Within a few months, we had renegotiated several different agreements.

In another instance, we had to tell a vendor we would not be paying them anymore because they had failed to deliver. They sued. We filed an action against them in return, and the squabble ended in arbitration. I felt confident about our claim, but I prayed throughout the dispute.

God, we're doing what we think is right here, but if we did do something wrong, make it clear and we will make it right.

I received a call that the arbitrator had ruled in our favor. He wanted to know how much money we wanted from the other side. The vindication was sweet, but here was an opportunity to pile drive this company that took advantage of us. The company owner called to congratulate me on the outcome and then asked how much it was going to cost him.

"There are no winners here," I said, knowing I could almost certainly put them out of business. "I don't have a figure yet, but know this: I will never, ever send any business your way. Do you understand?"

When I asked our finance department how much

the legal wrangling had cost us, the number came to $110,000. That was no small amount for a business running close to the wire like we were. I called our attorney and told him I wanted a significantly smaller amount back from the supplier.

"Brig, that's not going to even cover our fees," he said.

"I know," I said. "They're a small operation. I don't want to kill them, but I do want it to sting. And I want the check on my desk within twenty-four hours." It was there the next day.

By the time we settled our problematic contract issues, we had saved around half a million dollars a year—almost twice the amount we had paid out in severance to our departing employees. I felt that God was affirming our efforts to operate with integrity and take care of others, even during challenging circumstances.

There was one more unexpected boost that encouraged me. Our incoming CFO had been incredulous about the way our badly needed capital was frozen, if not lost forever, in that stalled auction rate security fund. He penned a letter about the situation to the Michigan attorney general.

Two weeks later, we got a letter from his office—our money was going to be released.

I didn't ask for all the details. I was just glad it had been satisfactorily resolved. To me it was more of a cause for relief than a reason to throw a party. I wasn't impressed when I got a call from the bank telling me they were going to send the check over with balloons and a cake.

As far as I was concerned, it was their misman-agement that had left us in jeopardy in the first place. I told them they could keep the party favors—a simple check would be enough. I did smile, however, when it arrived. I went to our IT director and told her she now had the money needed to refit the corporate office with updated computers and software.

* * *

Everyone is on their own personal ship. Are you happy with where your boat is taking you? Is your ship safe in port, or are you headed out into the deep blue water? "Ships are safe in port, but that's not what ships are built for." Your life is no different!

Years ago I read about some big sailing rigs that got caught by flat seas out in the middle of the ocean. Day after day, the ships sat, not moving. The crews became fidgety and hungry—so hungry that they decided to eat some of the horses on the boats. Then they threw the horse heads overboard. The following morning, the captains woke to find the horse heads bobbing next to the boat, so they named this area the "Horse Head Latitudes."

After waiting much too long to act, one of the

captains dropped a lifeboat in the water. He put the ship's big anchor into the lifeboat, and the crew rowed out as far as the anchor chain would let them. They would drop the anchor from the lifeboat ahead of the ship. As the ship retrieved the anchor, the ship would move toward the anchor, thus moving the boat forward.

If Bob Saari had been on the boat, he would've been screaming his approval in his thick Finnish accent: "Do something! Even if it's wrong!" We cannot move forward into the deep blue water if we remain stagnant on flat seas.

CHAPTER THIRTEEN

Are You an Asset or a Liability?

DURING THE HEIGHT of the battle to keep Two Men and a Truck above water, there was an endless round of meetings—fires to put out and fires to light under people. I had staff coming in and out of my office all day. The amount of time I had to think clearly seemed to be like my fuse: short. I didn't have the luxury of just shooting the breeze.

I began to identify the people who came in to see me not by their title or longevity but by their attitude. Were they here to pour into me or drain me? Were they a help or a hindrance? I imagined a flashing sign above their heads. It read "Liability" or "Asset." In meetings, I would glance around the room and make a mental note about each person—*liability... liability... asset... not sure yet... asset...liability.*

The seeds of this evaluation had been sown a few years earlier when I drove my boys, Jake and Brycen, to our hunting camp in the Upper Peninsula. This was not going to be a typical family vacation with lots of goofing around and downtime. They were at an age for their first "man's" trip—a work trip before the start of deer season to prep for hunts later in the year.

We still had fun—but a different kind of fun.

Instead of beach balls, sun umbrellas, and towels, we were packing firearms, four-wheelers, and chainsaws. The weather forecast was immaterial: hot, cold, wet, dry, snow, or mosquitoes—it didn't matter. Whatever the elements were going to throw at us, we had to get out and get things done.

To prepare them, I explained the difference between an asset and a liability. "An asset is something that helps you accomplish a goal," I said. "A liability is something that takes away from the resources that help you attain the goal." They nodded, understanding as I continued.

"You guys are a question mark at this point," I explained. "Will you be an asset or a liability? If you are constantly arguing? Liability. Not picking up your stuff or cleaning up after yourself? Liability. Helping to stack split wood without complaining? Asset. Doing the dishes without being asked? Asset. Starting the sauna and filling the water buckets—asset. This trip is going to be a learning experience. I will call it as I see it during the next three days."

To their credit, it went well. The boys did great. Given the challenge to achieve something, they stepped up. For every liability I called, I got three assets. We had a great time and still talk about that trip to this day.

Word spread around the Two Men and a Truck home office about me being on the lookout for assets. It soon became known that I valued ass-kickers—people who would get in there and get things done.

Ass-kickers stayed on task. They did the boring but essential things and did them well. They took notes. They didn't just come with issues—they came prepared with suggestions for solutions.

They were engaged in the details and could grind through the minutia of a challenge.

They didn't just look out for their own interests. They didn't make alliances or cliques in the office to try to advance their careers. They brought people together. When an ass-kicker came into a meeting, I felt the room get smarter and brighter. When I saw an ass-kicker, I thought of those old commercials for BASF from back in the '90s: "We don't make the products you buy. We make the products you buy better."

Being seen as an ass-kicker became a quiet source of pride around the office, and our franchisees picked up on it too. One sent me a baseball hat reading "I'm an Ass Kicker" on the front. I loved it. We even had an "Ass Kickers Hall of Fame" for a time, with photos and stories of home office and franchise staff who had earned the title. Not everyone appreciated the redneck term, however, so to be politically correct, we changed the signage on the wall to "Heavy Lifters Way." But I still use "Ass Kicker" and will not give it up!

That whatever-it-takes attitude is a key part of

what has driven Two Men and a Truck to year-over-year growth for more than a decade—a remarkable achievement for any business. This mindset has earned us top-tier rankings in publications such as *Entrepreneur*, *Forbes*, *Franchise Times*, and *Franchise Business Review*. We've been positively featured on programs such as *The 700 Club* and Fox News.

Despite all the behind-the-scenes operational challenges we have faced—along with some of the self-made problems we've dealt with—we are really, really good at what we do: moving people and their possessions. It's not just a question of loading everything into a big truck and driving down the road.

We are not simply relocating people; we reposition them in their lives. They could be moving somewhere they have long dreamed of, or they could be escaping a nightmare. The move may be a cause of celebration: a marriage, job promotion, expanded family, or the construction of their perfect home. It could also be the source of intense sadness, such as a divorce, job loss, death, or health crisis.

When I sold insurance, part of my job was to help the customer understand what they would want if their lives got thrown into havoc. At Two Men and a Truck, we come into people's lives when their worlds are up in the air—most of it in boxes.

We pick up not just furniture and boxes but tokens of our customers' lives. We transport their memories.

ARE YOU AN ASSET OR A LIABILITY?

In one sense, their lives are exposed to us as we lift and haul. This can be awkward at times. On more than one occasion, our crews have moved a mattress only to find some intimate items tucked away and forgotten underneath. We have also come across enough handguns to arm a small militia.

In such moments, we're discreet. We casually mention that there is something on the floor they might like to deal with as we take the mattress and frame out to the truck, giving them a chance to tidy up before we return. We don't turn a blind eye to everything though. A few years back, a franchise called the home office wanting to know what to do because they had come across a stash of child pornography. I told them to call the police, which they did. There's a difference between preserving someone's privacy and protecting others from a living hell.

It has been surprising to discover how many people keep sizable sums of money under their mattresses. For example, while moving an elderly man's bed, a team found a thick roll of one-hundred-dollar bills bundled by two rubber bands and covered in dust. The money had obviously been there a long time.

As our guys walked a box spring out of the house, our mover tossed the thick roll of bills into the customer's hand. The mover winked as the man's jaw dropped. It would have been easy for one of the guys to pocket the money without anyone knowing.

But integrity is something our company stresses from day one. People in transition are entrusting us with their valuables. There is a vulnerability associated with letting someone else move your belongings, and we consider that a sacred trust.

On another occasion, a team had just finished loading up and prepared to roll out. At the last second, one of them spotted something as he crossed the lawn. Bending down, he found a diamond ring in the grass. When he brought it to the woman of the house and asked if it was hers, she burst into tears. She had lost the ring—which had tremendous sentimental value— while mowing the yard a couple of years before.

There have been some very special, very human moments in the midst of all the hustle. During my franchise days in the Upper Peninsula, I went back to the truck to grab the clipboard and paperwork after moving a piano into a woman's home. As I walked back to the house, I could hear a beautiful melody spilling out through the windows. I imagined the woman was testing the piano to make sure it was still in tune after the move. But when I stepped inside, she was standing against a wall, quietly crying.

My young Two Men and a Truck employee was seated at the piano, his back brace undone and his gloves set on top of the baby grand as he ran his hands over the keys. I swelled with pride as we finished the paperwork—I shook her hand and bathed in his beautiful music.

"Hey, I didn't know you could do that," I said as we returned to the truck.

He shrugged. "You never asked."

He didn't look like a pianist to me. Then again, he probably didn't look like a mover to some of our customers either. Slightly built, he was working with Two Men and a Truck while he went through medical school.

Each move has helped us fine-tune our approach. We know that when we arrive at a move site, we need to have a toolbox of talents—from walking through the house and drawing a mental schematic, to deciding what to move first, to building our base for the load. From examining how each piece will lock in and strap down with the other pieces to handling the customers' emotions.

Making a good first impression is essential. That's why we are insistent that trucks are swept clean and pads folded and neatly stacked when we open up the back. That gives people confidence that we will treat their things carefully. It's also why there is no smoking allowed in the back of the trucks. We don't want customers turning up their noses at a stale smell that makes them question whether their things will be handled with care.

Our approach is summed up by one of our company core values, which my family created. We call it The Grandma Rule˚. It means we treat everyone the way we'd want our grandmas treated. It's a message we drive home in one of the posters we have hanging in most Two Men and a Truck offices. On the poster is a photo of Grandma Eberly along with a description of The Grandma Rule˚.

If you're going to evaluate how others measure up—rating them as an asset or a liability—you have to judge yourself by the same standard. Are you an asset at work? Do you make the meeting brighter and smarter when you take a seat at the table?

Let's take this further. Are you an asset or a liability when you walk through the doorway of your own home? An asset or a liability as a spouse, a parent, or a roommate? How about as a neighbor or a spectator at one of your kids' games?

The time came when I had to take an honest look at the different areas of my life. Though I prided myself on being a true asset at work, I had to ask myself: *What was I like at home? Were Fran and the kids getting the most out of me, or was I a drag?* Looking back, I had to admit that all too often, they were getting the left-overs. After my busy day at the office, I was running on fumes.

I was tired and not keen on being in crowded places. I didn't want to go out and do stuff. I just wanted to be left alone. I missed many adventures and some significant opportunities to make memories. Realizing that I might be considered more of a liability on the home front, I determined to be more proactive and get more involved in everyone's lives.

Then I started looking at other parts of my life. Was I an asset to our Two Men and a Truck franchises? How about at the gym? What about at church?

Did I bring anything positive to my interactions with people I didn't know? I'd read about how if you smile at anyone, they will likely smile back. I decided to try it. Turns out, it's true. I began to make smiling a habit.

I also found that setting out to be an asset to others was beneficial for me. Some days I would get hit by a bout of despair. It was nothing like the heaviness I had experienced before I gave my life to God, but an undeniable sense of the blues could come out of nowhere and leave me feeling flat.

Part of it was probably just exhaustion—too many nights of broken sleep juggling all the things that needed to be done. I would look at my schedule and my to-do list and start to feel overwhelmed. In that kind of a depleted state, it wouldn't take much—maybe just a cutting remark from someone—and I could slide sideways into a full-blown pity party wrapped with a big bow of self-doubt.

When I spoke about that to Mike Winter from CBMC, he offered some advice: "If you want to feel better, you need to get your mind off yourself and do something nice for someone."

"Like what?" I asked.

"I don't know," he said. "Randomly help someone with some money or offer your time. Just look for an opportunity."

That exchange came to mind when I walked into a Meijer grocery store after work one day. I felt as if I were wearing one of those lead vests they put on you before you get an X-ray. My breathing was shallow and my heart was fluttering. I tend to talk to myself when I'm alone during these moods. (I also swear quietly to myself out loud or in my thoughts.)

As I grabbed a grocery cart and pushed it through the entrance, I was met by an older lady who was the greeter. She was smiling way too much—at the level of being a public nuisance. With the feeling of benching too much weight, I forced myself to squeeze out a smile and return her hello. "It's not her issue," I whispered to myself.

I was grumbling about what kind of difference there was between an organic banana and a regular one while I consulted the list Fran had given me. My attention was soon drawn to a grocery cart diagonal to mine in the produce section. It was half-full of groceries with a child in the seat.

She was a beautiful baby with the most piercing light blue eyes. Close by was a little girl I assumed to be her sister, about four years old. She had an energy that made me smile despite my mood. She reminded me of those store signs that warn parents to look after their kids, or they will be given a free puppy and a cappuccino. I wondered what she had done with the free puppy. The girls' mom was very kind and patient with her.

Then the thought came to me. *Buy her groceries.* I immediately told myself there was no way in hell I was paying for her groceries. I turned my cart and went in the other direction.

But as I randomly worked my way down the aisles, I found myself repeatedly crossing paths with this mom and her girls. The older girl continued to chatter away, like an old forty-five record playing too fast. I looked for her cappuccino mustache.

All the while, the little girl in the cart sat content and quiet, head up, just taking in the world. She never made a peep. If she had listened hard, she might have caught the inner dialogue I was having with myself, or maybe the Holy Spirit.

Buy the groceries.

No!

If you see her again in the next aisle, it's a sign you're supposed to buy her groceries.

Fine!

In the hope of avoiding them, I decided to skip four aisles and come back for what I needed a bit later. Surprise, surprise—I turned the corner and, *bam*, there they were again.

No way. I can't walk up to a young woman who is a complete stranger and say I want to buy her groceries. She'll think I'm some kind of pervert and scream for security. My dazed face will be on the local news as another businessman who lost it. I'm not doing it!

Buy her groceries.

Even I know when I'm losing an argument, so I finally gave in—with one final caveat. I'd pay if she ended up checking out when I did.

The woman and her daughters were nowhere in sight when I pulled into my checkout lane. I smiled triumphantly until the mother pushed their cart into a line three lanes away. "Shit," I mumbled to myself, admitting defeat. I left my cart, and I walked over to her with my heart pounding.

"Excuse me, ma'am?" After talking to myself all day in my head, the actual sound of my voice seemed weird.

"Yes?"

"Can I ask a favor?" I said. "You would do me a huge favor if you would let me buy your groceries."

"What?" she asked. There was a hint of a smile on her face.

"It's hard to explain," I answered, "but it would mean a lot if I could do this." Now I started to worry that she might be offended, that I thought she was poor. Or maybe she'd dismiss it as a creepy old guy's pick-up line before she screamed for security.

"Sure," she said. "What a blessing for my family."

Relieved, I asked her to pull her cart in front of mine. I quietly told the young cashier to run both of our carts through so I could pay at the end. But my internal dialogue hadn't quite finished.

Man, she has a ton of groceries. . . . Shut up!

As our groceries were bagged, the young lady told me that she and her husband had finally managed to find a sitter for the upcoming weekend. They were going to Holland on Lake Michigan for the honeymoon they'd never had. They didn't have any money, but they would look for free things to do there.

"That's awesome," I told her as I felt the lead vest slide off my back and hit the floor. I looked into the crystal eyes of the baby in the cart. She broke into a smile, showing the whitest newly grown bottom teeth. For a moment, I could have been looking into the face of Jesus. The lady gave me a hug of appreciation before trotting off with her daughters and their groceries.

My drive to Meijer's had been full of heaviness and apprehension. My drive home was one of lightness and appreciation. I realized that this young mom's burdens made my issues seem embarrassingly minute. I wondered how many more opportunities to help other people—and myself for that matter—would present themselves once I allowed my focus to shift.

CHAPTER FOURTEEN

Owning Your Space

JUST RECENTLY, I heard Joel Osteen on the radio explain how your life is like a building and your friends are scaffolding. As you grow, that scaffolding needs to come down, and new scaffolding needs to go up in other areas of your life. That does not mean you do not appreciate old friends, but it may mean you're no longer as close as you once were. And at the same time, you are the scaffolding on someone else's building.

As we change, so do the people we look up to and the people we want to emulate. Two Men and a Truck's current president, Randy Shacka, will tell our movers that they are the average of their five best friends, an idea initially coined by American entrepreneur Jim Rohn. I love this message. Some of my closest friends are people I didn't even know five or ten years ago.

One of them is Pastor Coye Bouyer, a Southern Baptist preacher and church planter who grew up in Lansing. The Rev—as we've come to call him—had a full-ride, four-year scholarship at Western Michigan University in track. After earning his undergraduate degree, he attended Dallas Seminary where he received a master's in theology. He returned to Lansing to start a small church, turning down a high-dollar job as the associate pastor of a Dallas megachurch.

I met Pastor Bouyer at a Lenten lunch at our office. His wife had come to sing. I arrived late and sat in the back of our conference room. My hair was still smoking from wrapping up one of our many "firefighting" meetings during the economic crisis of '08. I sat next to Pastor Bouyer, and he asked if I ran the business.

"Yes," I replied.

"Can I have lunch with you?" he asked. "I have business questions about my church."

He could not have asked at a better time. I was razor-sharp with what we were going through. After we talked about business, I started asking Pastor Bouyer faith-related questions. He helped me bring biblical perspective into my life. That scaffolding will not come down any time soon.

I have also been greatly influenced by my involvement with business groups such as the Young Presidents' Organization (YPO); Business Leaders for Michigan (BLM); the Catholic business group, Legatus; and the Christian Business Men's Connection (CBMC). There have also been informal groups such as The Ironmen. The name was derived from Scripture: "Iron sharpens iron, and one man sharpens another" (Proverbs 27:17 ESV).

I give time to those who enrich my life, to people who are helping me become better—not just as a businessman and leader but as a husband, father, family member, and friend. I don't have time for gossipers, grumblers, or people who have a victim mentality.

Wisely allocating my time has meant distancing myself from people who may not share my values. It's not that I am judging or looking down on anyone. I am glad to have the opportunity to talk with them about how we might see the world differently. But I have only so much time. I want to invest in relationships that make me better so that, as a result, I can be a better person for everyone else.

Bluntly, there are occasions when I kick a friend to the curb. I'm not talking about someone who is down on his luck. I mean the guy who doesn't honor my marriage, my faith, or my work ethic. People who are constantly negative. People who don't celebrate the good things happening in my life, or theirs for that matter.

For example, I was at a friend's hunting camp with a bunch of guys who decided to watch some porn. I wasn't going to give a lecture, but that's just not my thing. I took my beer outside to sit and watch the stars. A couple of other guys came out and joined me, and we got to talking about life and what really matters.

The group I share my time with is a blend—a few are people from my past but primarily it's those representing where I want to go. It would shock some of my new friends if they could have seen me back in the day. I say all of this for several reasons.

First, as you read this book, I hope you'll assess who and what you are surrounding yourself with. What scaffolding is currently in your life? Is it attached to the correct building? Do you need to move it?

This matters because of a concept I have adopted: You must continue evolving and growing. There will always be a new past, a new present, and a new future. Making the right choice in tough decisions becomes much clearer when you understand that each day is full of change and possibility.

Life is full of obstacles, challenges, disappointments, and sorrows. There is no escaping this truth. But life can also be full of successes, excitement, fulfillment, and happiness. The moment you grasp this is when your focus changes—you will never settle for remaining in the muck.

This story plays out each time I get the opportunity to talk with our Two Men and a Truck movers and drivers.

Recently, Randy (the current president of Two Men and a Truck) and I were in Philadelphia on a Tuesday morning, standing in what could be the dingiest, darkest, and dampest office I have ever seen.

What the hell? I thought. It was worse than the first office we had after the business left the confines of our kitchen table in Okemos thirty-two years ago— the shed off my grandma's barn. It had no bathroom. Sally, our lone customer service representative at the

196

time, had to use the gas station restroom up the street. The movers took a whizz behind the barn.

This Philly location flew against everything our system had worked so hard for. Our franchisee at the time said this was a temporary location until their new office was complete. I made a mental note: *We will deal with this later.*

Randy and I started our morning meeting in the lobby of a Hampton Inn. I rolled my eyes when I saw Randy with his chipper smile, pulling his bag and holding a cup of coffee. We were wearing the same thing, again—a black Two Men and a Truck polo shirt, khaki pants, black belt, and black shoes.

It doesn't help that Randy and I barely push five feet, eight inches and we both have short blond hair and blue eyes. We looked like two upper management action figures who just busted out of our doll boxes in the management aisle at a franchise store. Maybe no one would notice.

We were there to honor how well the franchise was doing. They had strong customer satisfaction scores and move numbers trending above company averages. Randy would talk about how we were doing system-wide, and I would offer perspective and history of the company.

As everyone came into the room, I liked the vibe. I could tell this franchise team was close, from the way they talked about sports to how they engaged in horseplay. There was lots of laughter. It was the same sense of family we found in all the best franchises as we made our way around the country giving these presentations.

The older movers were like work-uncles or big brothers to the younger ones. The older CSRs were like big sisters or moms, calling out movers by name and scolding them as needed, telling them to tuck their shirts in or watch their mouths. It made me smile to see this dynamic, remembering my time on the trucks with my kids, who all worked for the company at some stage.

Like all our franchises, the Philly group was diverse. All shapes and sizes and a range of ages. A few were just pushing twenty, but most were in their late twenties to mid-thirties. Then there was a handful of outliers—guys in their mid- to upper-forties. While some may have had more experience, I had an appreciation for them all—anyone who makes it beyond four months working on the trucks has some moxie. You can't survive the job without it.

With nearly four thousand trucks hitting the pavement at the height of summer, our movers and drivers experience a lot of drama—and even a bit of trauma—on the job. Over the years, we've heard countless stories of our movers pulling people from blazing vehicles; rescuing people from cars sinking in lakes, ponds, and rivers; and helping save people from burning homes. This is not part of our training but more of a testament to the type of people we attract.

Are all our employees like this? No, but franchise locations like this one in Philly have their fair share. It can be seen in the faces of many who are part of this group. Some of the others, I am confident, will find it inside themselves while they continue to grow at our company.

Some of the people in this franchise team probably thought I came from money—that my family had already been wealthy when we started Two Men and a Truck. The stories that float around can be funny. Grandma Sorber overheard someone say in her assisted living home that a Jewish syndicate had started our company. That angered her—I couldn't stop laughing.

"I know what some of you are thinking," I said when it was my turn to speak. "*Man, is he old. Wow, this dude is small.*"

That got a few chuckles. Then I told them to hold up a minute—I was moving furniture before most of them were born.

I recalled my story bit by bit. Growing up without a lot of money. Parents divorcing. Working moves for extra cash. Taking five years to get a four-year degree that I couldn't explain to anyone and still have never used. My girlfriend and I finding out we were pregnant and then getting married. Having a baby, needing to take government welfare, and working multiple jobs to stay just above the poverty line. No insurance. Paying off student loans and somehow finding enough money to buy our first house for $15,000—an old dump that we wrestled into a home.

By now, I had their attention, so I asked my favorite question: "Whose goal was it in life to be a mover?" Nobody raised their hands. "When you were playing in your front yards before the streetlights went on, you didn't raise your hand and yell, 'It's my turn to be the mover!'" That got a laugh.

"Well, me neither," I told them.

Some of them relaxed a little, so I told them I would share some thoughts with them. I reminded them again that I had been around this job long before many of them were born, so I have witnessed several trends.

"Some of it might sting," I said, "but I am going to talk straight because I love you."

Sure, I didn't know them personally, but I had been where they were, and I had worked with many others just like them. I truly cared about them.

"For starters," I began, "I can put the group of guys in this room into one of three buckets." No matter where I am speaking, or the size of the audience, these buckets hold true.

"First bucket—you are using Two Men and a Truck to grow," I said. "Maybe to pay for school or maybe you're saving money to move somewhere else to start your career. Or your goal could be to move up within Two Men and a Truck."

I explained that two out of three managers across our system had started on the trucks or working the phones. Almost half of the franchise owners had begun the same way. Many of them did not have college educations.

"To sum it up, you have a plan. You are using us to better your situation. This is where we want you. Our goal is to be part of the stepping-stone in your career."

Then came bucket two. "You don't know how the hell you ended up becoming a mover," I said, looking around. "You're sitting there thinking, *I had great expectations for my life. How did this happen to me?* I'll come back to you in a minute."

"Those in bucket three," I said. "Excuse my language, but you don't give a shit. You're not even listening to me right now." That always seems to get one or two guys to straighten up.

"Don't worry, you're not hurting my feelings. I have been around you all my life. Remember, I've been moving furniture since before most of you were born, so let me tell you what's going to happen to you.

"You will jump from one job to another. These lateral job changes are not because you are working a career path—you are simply chasing what you think is easy money or work. You wander from place to place in your profession and relationships.

"A profession and a relationship to you is like

buying a new car. When new, you are filled with excitement and energy. As soon as you lose your euphoria, you drop what you have and look for what's new again—never investing in what you have. This lack of dedication leads to lateral moves and leaves a trail of broken relationships, never finding lasting meaning and gratification in either.

"You will do this until your mid- to upper-thirties, give or take a few years. You'll eventually lift your head from your day-to-day and notice that your good friends are gone. Maybe even some of your family members.

"By the time you realize you haven't built a solid career, or a life for that matter, you're toast. You are neck-deep in a quagmire, living until your end days hand-to-mouth. Only by the grace of God will you have the time to turn that around. Think I'm kidding? Remember, I've been around long before many of you were breathing air. I've seen this over and over.

"You are all here in this room. Every group is represented. I just don't know who is in what bucket."

By now, I had most people's attention. I asked how many were currently attending or had previously been to college. As was typically the case, it turned out that about a third had at least taken some college courses. Many of those people were the bucket two guys. I now homed in on them.

"Why do you go to college?" I asked. "How does that work?"

"You take classes, get a degree, then look for a job," someone hollered from the back.

"You take classes, get a degree, and then look for a job. That's right," I said. "You take the classes, you learn a bunch of stuff, and you spit it out on a test. If you have learned enough, they give you a piece of paper that says Billy learned this stuff. Then you take that piece of paper and wave it around to companies looking for people who have learned those things. Then, after a few interviews, you may get hired.

"What's the difference here at Two Men and a Truck? In this job, you will learn how to manage people, time, money, and equipment. We have over four hundred online courses you can take. There is mobility. You can become drivers, move consultants, managers, even a franchisee.

"Again, we have many franchisees who do not have college educations. Many of these people have multiple locations and run million-dollar businesses. Do they all know everything about IT, human resources, or finance? Nope, but guess what? They hire people who did go to college for those things.

"Here's the thing—these franchisees treated their early years working as movers, CSRs, drivers, and managers like it was their college. Your time here, if you apply yourself, is not wasted. However, opportunity is not a glittering diamond. It looks more like a well-worn Carhartt coat and muddy boots."

I told the group about the commercials that really make me sick: those beer ads with beautiful, skinny young people wearing form-fitting, expensive clothes. They leave their trendy corner offices in an upscale city looking tired and angry, even though it's always still light outside. No one seems to work a full day, I've noticed.

They walk into a hip little bar where they meet up with their skinny, good-looking friends with their bleached, straight-teeth smiles, and everyone commiserates about how bad their day has been. Then they open their beers and they are magically whisked to a tropical paradise where they find themselves on a beach in their skimpy bathing suits.

"That's pure bullshit," I said. "There is no such place. The people who make it are the people who grind.

"Nobody owes you a damn thing," I went on. "Nobody. Not your parents, uncles, aunts, or your grandparents. They owe you nothing. Local, state, and federal governments owe you jack. Two Men and a Truck owes you nothing. God Himself owes you precisely nothing! Be grateful He allows you to breathe air. You owe all to God.

"If you feel you're owed something and don't get it, guess what? You have now become a victim. Victims are held captive because someone else holds them as a prisoner.

"Fact is, life is unfair. Maybe you had a coach or a teacher who screwed you over. Maybe you had a parent who mistreated you. Perhaps there was a girl-friend who cheated, you felt short-changed at work, or somehow the government did not come through for you. Get over it!

"I've found that most people didn't wake up trying to figure out how to screw with my life.

"Most of them couldn't manage their own, let alone deliberately try to mess with mine.

"Whenever you start to feel sorry for yourself, remind yourself that you are blessed. If you slept with a roof over your head last night, if you have running water and a toilet that flushes, if you are not starving to death, if you love someone and someone loves you back—you have it better than ninety-five percent of the people in the world. Think about it.

"Do you know what the average daily wage is in the world right now? Two dollars. People are lined up on the Mexican border, risking it all to sneak into this country—we need our military and a wall to hold them back. People are literally dying to sneak in here to eat our scraps.

"We have all been dealt a hand of cards. Some hands are better than others. That's just the way it is. Quit peeking at someone else's hand—that is none of your damn business. Don't get sucked into what popular songs and the media say your hand should look like—it's none of their damn business.

"Play the hand you were dealt the best you can."

I then told them to look at the floor covered with office-gray carpet squares. "For some of you, your area of influence makes up just one square," I said. "As a mover, your job may be to fold the pads after the move, sweep out the back of the truck, and help the driver to safely back the truck up in the driveway. That's it. We have over ten thousand employees at the height of our busy season. Be the best at what you do. Own that square!

"If you show up ready to work every day and you're the best at that one square—your small area of influence—in time, management may offer you the opportunity to be a driver, a trainer, or an estimator. Your one square is now two squares." I spread my feet accordingly.

"Your area of influence just doubled. That, guys, is called a career. Some of you might say that the pay to be a driver is not worth the extra hassle and responsibility of driving. That's bullshit. It's no different than going to college and moving from freshman to sophomore. Of course it's harder. It's supposed to be. Remember, nobody owes you a damn thing. So when opportunity calls, step up."

I offered ideas on how to be ready. Prepare for work the night before and have a clean uniform folded before going to bed. Have a plan on how to get to work. Have bus fare ready or gas in the car. Text the buddy who is going to pick you up. Be proactive. Start the day in front of the eight ball, not behind it. In other words, don't start out from a difficult or unfortunate position if you don't have to. "If you find yourself in a bad mood when you get to work," I advised, "just shut up! Nobody cares about your bad mood. Only open your mouth after you have adjusted yourself.

"How many of you are still living at home?" I asked. About a third of the hands went up. "Clean your own damn room," I said with a grin. "You guys call yourself men, but you have someone else telling you to clean your rooms? Start doing your own laundry. Don't know how? YouTube it.

"When was the last time you brought a pizza home or took your family to dinner?

"If you think you are a man, start acting like one. Start branding yourself at work and home. Keep your car clean. Keep your yard clean. You've got a piece of shit car? Then have the cleanest piece of shit car on the block."

By the time I finished, I could gauge which bucket each guy was in by his response. The first bucket guys were nodding in agreement like a collection of bobble-heads. The second bucket guys looked back at me with wide eyes and open mouths, hope rising. The third bucket guys weren't engaged at all—who knows what they were thinking.

I shared some of my own mistakes at various points during this hard-nosed speech. I told them that I hoped they'd learn something from my mishaps and hard-earned lessons. I hoped they would realize they had more control over their lives than they thought.

"It took me to my mid-forties before I figured out the advice I've given you today," I said. "Let's not be afraid to learn from one another—to share the pitfalls of bad decisions and best practices in our daily lives. This will help to move us forward in every area."

I finished speaking like I did most times—simultaneously tired, pumped, and hopeful. Hopeful that a few might catch a spark that would ignite the fire of possibilities in their lives. Out in the parking lot, one of the team members—a fit-looking young guy—came up to Randy and me as we walked to our car. He seemed a bit nervous.

"I don't know how to talk to you," he said.

"How about English," I joked, trying to put him at ease. "What's up?"

"I . . . I . . . I needed to hear that," he said simply. I was pumped. *Yes!* I said to myself.

"Thanks," I replied. "Isn't it freeing that no one can permanently keep you back? Your destiny is in your hands. How many times do we feel like we are in a jail cell? We're screaming and pulling the bars, trying to open the door. But how about we simply push the door open and walk out?"

We talked some more, and it was clear that he really got it. He was moving forward, one carpet square at a time.

Moments like that—when you know you've helped at least one other person—are what it's all about.

Take the First Step

I FOUND MYSELF squinting in the summer sun, looking at a man standing on my roof. All I could see was the silhouette of his bowlegged body with a hammer hanging from his belt.

"Every house has issues, including yours," he began. "I'm sure they start small, at or near the foundation, but by the time they get up here, they're big. When you work up here all day, you see the adjustments they made in the roof to cover the mistakes they made below. Be off by a tenth of an inch down there and you could be off several inches up here."

I smiled, thinking that the roofer could be God talking about our lives. Jesus had been a carpenter—I let this thought linger. If our lives were houses, our roofs would be cockeyed. Can we ever make them straight? Can our lives be perfectly plumb? I don't think so.

I returned to the significance of Jesus' time as a carpenter. A sin-soaked, broken world influences our building materials and laborers. Constructing our lives under the world's influence is not wise, because we will one day be judged by a perfect God. But a perfect God always has a perfect plan. God sent His Son, Jesus, to cover our sins with His blood. In the end, through Christ, believers will be plumb in God's eyes.

Worry, anxiety, and fear will keep us in daily bondage if we give in to them. We will find ourselves trying to simply survive another day. We are given opportunities, however, to become better versions of ourselves as we travel through life. I have found that the possibilities for change, growth, fulfillment, and peace are all around us—but they don't just fall into our laps.

We must be willing to search for the answers that can navigate us toward peace and fulfillment. In the fifth chapter of the Gospel of John, Jesus found a man near the pool of Bethesda who had been disabled, completely unable to walk, for thirty-eight years.

Jesus asked him, "Do you want to be made well?"

The man replied, "Sir, I have no man to put me into the pool when the water is stirred up; but while I am coming, another steps down before me."

Jesus said to him, "Rise, take up your bed and walk." And immediately the man was made well, took up his bed, and walked.

It is interesting that Jesus had to tell the man to rise, pick up his bed, and walk after He healed him. I am curious if the man found it hard to use his healed legs. Maybe he sat back down on his bed a time or two. It's human nature to return to the familiar instead of taking on something new—even when the new is better. Sometimes it's easier to hold on to our old ways.

How many times do Christians know they are healed but still sit back down in their beds, so to speak? We may not be disabled, but we lean on old crutches that are no longer necessary after being saved. Do we harbor our insecurities, jealousies, and anger for years, even after we have been made well?

In Mark 3, Jesus healed a man's paralyzed hand in the synagogue. This man had somehow gotten by with one hand his whole life. Thanks to Jesus, he now had two useful hands. We can't assume he went on his way, getting one hundred percent out of both hands. He had to learn how to use his new hand in conjunction with the other. Since he had grown accustomed to doing without one hand, this change may not have come naturally. He had to break old habits and learn new ones.

However, I'm confident that, in time, the formerly disabled man who picked up his bed and walked would eventually toss his old bed. And the man whose hand was restored in the synagogue would ultimately use both hands to their fullest. But it took work. Likewise, as believers, we are blessed—but we need to be willing to adapt to God's blessings. We must let go of our old ways and take risks to do things differently.

We cannot sleepwalk through this life hoping things will get better. We need to take control of the things we can control, no matter how small they seem. I think again about the ships in the Horse Head Latitudes. They would drop their anchors from the lifeboats and then pull them back in, just to move the boats when the seas were flat. Or the mover who woke up one day and made the decision to become a driver and, by so doing, increased his area of influence and built his resume.

How about looking in the mirror and smiling at yourself and saying out loud, "You suck!" Not in a self-deprecating way but in a tongue-in-cheek way to tell yourself, "I'm going to do better today."

Our daily choices will either lessen or expand the number of degrees keeping us off-center. As I grew in faith, I realized God's Word is my center, my true north. When I began adjusting my personal and business life toward His direction, I made more proactive decisions. Each one might not have been a game-changer in itself, but bundled together over time, my decisions moved the needle closer to the center.

I started with the closest people in my life and realized some of them didn't make me better. I became very good at slowly backing out of relationships that did not honor God, my marriage, or my work ethic.

What about TV, movies, music, and the internet? I've chosen to be off Facebook altogether and I'm very particular about what I listen to or watch. I have enough drama in my life to manage—I don't need to watch it manufactured for my entertainment. All that stuff is junk food for the brain.

With all the time I've saved, I've begun reading more about things that matter, using the internet as a tool to gather useful information. As a by-product, I've become proficient at fixing many things around the house. Things I never would have attempted before.

The challenges and issues I had in the past were not horrible memories to be buried but experiences to be mined for answers to present-day problems. If your life has been loaded with struggles and challenges, you also have life experiences to draw on. Don't waste the pain.

The same holds true for people. Looking back, I learned just as much—if not more—from the people who hurt me. By dredging up some of these people and their actions, I was able to sift the diamonds from the mud.

How did they hurt me, and how did that make me feel? What could have been said or done to make a better outcome? I asked myself.

Then I asked myself the really tough question. *I know how that makes me feel—am I doing that to others?*

Don't ever forget the pain of being hurt. Let the pain make you more aware of the feelings of others. Own the pain you felt, and use the lessons learned as an antidote for similar challenges. You don't want to go through life carrying past hurt around, but you can exercise caution and wisdom as you move forward. When practiced, this becomes an easy exercise that gives you power over situations and people who hurt you.

In Scripture, King David, Joseph, Moses, and Job are just a few men who became great by overcoming and learning from their challenges. Just like these men in the Bible, we won't learn from our struggles if we sleepwalk through life. Often, difficult people and challenges are allowed into our lives to season us for later greatness.

If you mine the diamonds buried in your hurt, you will gain wisdom and discernment—accumulating emotional and intellectual equity to be invested in present-day challenges. Proverbs 16:16 states, "How much better to get wisdom than gold! And to get understanding is to be chosen rather than silver."

People who sleepwalk through life carry a weighted pain sack over their shoulders. Mine the diamonds from your misery, pocket the jewels, and leave the bag on the side of the road.

In many cases, when our business suffered or my personal life felt bankrupt, I avoided many headaches by not looking out the window for excuses. Instead, I looked into the mirror for accountability.

Rather than sitting on our hands and waiting for the environment to change, we can empower ourselves by working on what we can control. Our environment is constantly changing, but it's better to be working in it and changing with it. The alternative is to remain flat-footed, waiting to dive in until the time is right. However, if we wait, we get discouraged, defeated, and feel helpless—we eventually become victims.

When we become victims, we hand over the keys of our life to those who have angered us, let us down, or somehow cheated us. In most cases, these key holders have no clue they are holding us captive—they are just living their everyday lives while we seethe in bitterness and disappointment.

Many people are frustrated, angry, and detached. Our country is greatly divided into a few camps, and the world is becoming more hostile. I question how much we can accomplish in big groups of same-way thinkers.

What if we worked on ourselves by controlling the things we can control on a micro level and finding our true north? In doing so, we can make our area of influence the best it can be.

Titus 3:1–3 states, "Remind them to be submissive to rulers and authorities, to be obedient, to be ready for every good work, to speak evil of no one, to avoid quarreling, to be gentle, and to show perfect courtesy toward all people. For we ourselves were once foolish, disobedient, led astray, slaves to various passions and pleasures, passing our days in malice and envy, hated by others and hating one another" (ESV).

Recall the three buckets mentioned in the last chapter. Throughout my life, I've spent time in every one of those buckets. There have been moments when I simply didn't care—I wasn't interested in investing in school, the early parts of my career, or in my relationships.

I saw my friends moving forward and became cynical of their progress. I blamed my upbringing—even God—for the things I didn't have. It was a dark place.

Eventually I stepped out of bucket three to bucket two. I looked for ways to pull myself out of the funk. I concluded that my freedom would be found in wealth. I worked hard and took risks. After several years, I found myself in a place where wealth was achieved. What I found was disappointing—empty and unfulfilling.

When is enough, enough?

I knew that the idea of fulfillment as a result of making more money was a mirage, a distant oasis in the desert that I could faintly see through the shimmering heat. Having more money didn't enhance my marriage, make me a better friend, or a better employee at work.

I found my answers in my true-north relationship with Christ. From there, I stepped into bucket one. With newfound faith, I gave my life to Him. I put on His yoke. That means I am harnessed to Him as we work together at the same pace, for the same goals. I got in step with His rhythm.

Only then did I find peace in this crazy world.

God did not stare down at me with crossed arms, shaking His head. Instead, He lovingly worked to restore the Brig He first created. As time went by, my marriage strengthened, and I became a better dad and friend. Work became more fulfilling and exciting.

God did not wave a wand over my life to make it easier. He showed me I was deeply loved, ransomed by His Son's sacrifice on the cross. He then taught me to look deep into my past and the present day to answer life's challenges.

What bucket do you find yourself in currently? Maybe you're in bucket one—you've been nodding in agreement as you read this final chapter. In bucket two? I hope I helped make it clear that the answers to your anxiety and frustration are all around you. Bucket three? You're probably not reading this, but if for some reason you are, you can be saved.

I was.

Do you feel you are locked in a cell, and someone or something else dangles the keys? Are you exhausted from trying to pull the jail door open, only to realize it was never locked? Try simply pushing the door open and walking out. It is my prayer that you will find your true north.

I know my life's story in itself does not warrant a book more than any other person's. All our lives are different and unique. I found my true north in God, and by doing so, I was able to rip off the false labels other people gave me and even the labels I gave myself. This put me on a quest to search for and find peace.

May you find your true north as well. Remember, it starts with that first step forward.

Acknowledgments

THEY SAY IT TAKES a village to raise a child. Well, it most definitely takes a large metro area to put some sense of a book together from my thoughts, words, and actions.

My wife, Fran, and I met when I was a childish college student. After we married, I was still both of those things. When we had our first child, I thought I was the man of the family. But looking back, Fran was raising our child and simultaneously bringing me up as an adolescent. Of all the people in my life, no one has influenced me more. Fran loved me, was patient with me, and never gave up on me. Over the years, our life grafted together into one, and through that process, Fran poured her positive attitude, patience, and faith into me. When people ask me to speak and do interviews, or even to write this book, it's not really me they are after—it's what Fran put into me. Saying thank you in a book's acknowledgments section seems trite considering the magnitude of the impact she has had on my life. But thank you, and I love you, Fran.

To Alicia, our oldest daughter who reminds me there were three of us walking down the aisle to get married on that cold February day in Marquette:

ACKNOWLEDGMENTS

Thank you for your support and the time you put into this book. Your wisdom and sage advice are beyond your years (you get that from your mom). I appreciate your dry, witty humor. Thank you for the encouragement and laughter when I needed it.

To Jake, our middle child: We used every suggestion you made on this book, and there were several. Thank you for carving out the time as a newlywed, and from your dental practice, for the deep dive you took.

To Brycen, our youngest: You are the largest and the quietest of us Sorbers. When you talk, we listen. Thank you for reading the book and giving your detailed suggestions and thoughts. You told me to keep the book sharp and edgy and not to soften it to please others. Keep it real. We did. You helped form the book.

To my dad, Jim Sorber: You saved your best fathering for me when I really needed it. In many ways you were left behind as Mary Ellen, Melanie, Jon, and I rode the roller coaster of building TMT. You were never envious of the business; you were one of our biggest cheerleaders. In the same way, you were never concerned how you were portrayed in the book. You were only concerned that I might be exposing Fran and myself too much. During the writing process, you filled in my memory gaps from times in my youth. That not only helped the book but helped me make sense of some of the questions I had when I was younger. The book and my life were

ACKNOWLEDGMENTS

both improved by your input. Thanks, Dad.

To Randy Shacka, our president: These pages would never have been written without you. It was you who more than ten years ago first suggested I write a book. My ribs now have a permanent bruise from you jabbing me every time people mentioned that I should write a book. Being a constant listener of podcasts and avid book reader, you were key in laying out the format. You have been part of the fabric of Two Men and a Truck since you interned here when you were nineteen years old. You and I have an ongoing argument on who has held the most positions in the company—let's call it a draw. Your history with the company, and the survival of a handful of world wars that are fought growing a business, has made you a walking file of our company history. Thank you, Randy, for the countless meetings you have set up with editors and publishers. Thank you for helping with the monumental task of a major rewrite of this book, sentence by sentence, and word by word. You did this while serving as president of Two Men and a Truck, married with two children, and all that comes with those roles. In a single word: amazing.

To Jon Nobis, our CEO: With your leadership, you have taken Two Men and a Truck further than it has ever been. The brief time we spent as co-CEOs was very memorable, and the time we spent in prayer over Two Men and a Truck only strengthened my faith. You

221

rolled up your sleeves and dove into this book along with Randy and me. You have never been one to mince words about this business, and the same holds true about the book. You have always been a searcher for the truth, which leads to hard questions and demands straightforward answers. This has made a better business and a better book. Thank you.

To our franchisees: What can I say? We grew up together. Many of you are family to me. Some of you I wanted to grab by the neck: John and Jason Judson, Tim Lightner, Chad Arnold, Kyle Norcutt, just to name a few. But by the next week, I wanted to hug you. The contributions of all our franchisees were amazing. Without your risk and perseverance, there would be no Two Men and a Truck. The adventure we took together will be lived again in our memories when we are much older. All of us can honestly say that we gave it our all.

A special shout-out to Reverend Coye Bouyer of Kingdom Life Church in Lansing, Michigan. You mirror Christ more than anyone I know. Thank you for sharing your perspective, thoughts, and encouragement regarding this book. The Bible studies you have led at our office changed my life, as I am sure is true for many others in our group. You are one of my best friends.

To Father Mike Murray, our priest at St. Martha Parish in Okemos: You have been an amazing sounding board for the book and one of a few who picked me up, dusted me off, and pushed me forward as I worked my way to finishing this project. You were not only a priest to me but also an attorney and an author (and maybe a boxer, too, I'm not sure). Thank you, Father Mike.

To Andy Butcher: You were my first hire to help me put words on paper. You were a man who sought the truth by diving into news articles and interviewing several people mentioned in the book. You set the foundation of the book. Thank you for the dedication you put into the early stages of the process.

And finally I want to thank my mom, Mary Ellen Sheets; my sister, Melanie Bergeron; and my brother, Jon Sorber. Without each one of you, there would have been no Two Men and a Truck business. Each of you risked it all. You poured your lives into this business, and by doing so you launched several thousand careers. The foundation of our core values and mission statement were set early by you before we franchised. Like every business, our business went through many changes. As the company grew, change became a part of our lives. These changes, at times, were tough on our family. Roles changed and evolved, but we stayed the course and always put our customers and franchisees first. Thank you for all you have done, not only for the company but for me as a person. I love each one of you more than you know.